FROM THE
DEAD

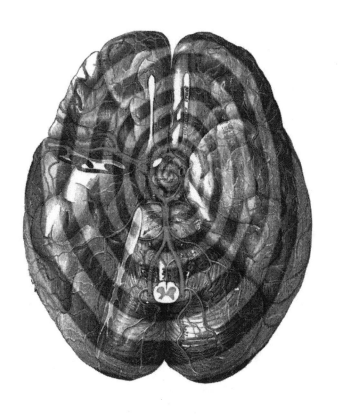

DEAD STAR PRESS

Acknowledgments

&

Dedications

For everyone who has supported us in our mission to bring more weird into the world and the incredible writers whose weird lies herein.

Karl Waldron, Megan and Stuart Shoen, Meredith and Bryan McCall, Amanda Riccardi and Joe Cimino, Gianfranco Rabaroza, Chris Donley, Stacey and William Hetrick, Donna White, Devin Robbins, Jared White, Brandon Ward, Timothy Armstrong, Natasha Head, Rebecca Riss, Tao Dong, L.W., Shane Kline, Gail Messler, JoLynn McClintock, Suli and Diego Apodaca, Ron Larson, Dajo and TJ, Jacob Bense, Christine Volk, Ryan Evans, Nikki Behr, Lori Arduini, Kerrie and Ryan Kline, Michael Drane, Rebecca Kuligowski, Aimee and Jason Wokutch, Stephen Waddell, Tom Prefling, David Alvarez, Jen Hoke, Jamie Chapman, Janet Sabol, Kristen and Chris Ottena, Alyssa Hernandez, Breena Bearce, Sebastien Reyes, Marie and David Turko, The Greenwalds, The Newcomers, and

Andrea and Ariella Nova.

TABLE OF CONTENTS

1.

THE GRAY AREA: OR IS IT THE GREY AREA?

(MR. GRAY IS MR. GREY)

BY

EDWIN LEE CANFIELD

What is the color of a TV tuned to a dead channel? When there were only a handful of broadcasting stations, it was sometimes a hypnotizing, visually bursting, and scrambling of static and noise filled with the colors of black and white and every shade of gray in between.

What is the color of a TV tuned to a dead channel currently? A black mirror? Black is the absence of light and, therefore, the absence of color. Are there any dead channels now? Digital signals can become degraded for a number of reasons, including several types of interference and latency as the signal travels some 22,223 miles. Typically, this results in the inconvenience of a jumpy, pixelated mutation of the image and sound. Word falling. Photo falling. Glitch. When the signal is lost completely, we are back to the black mirror and the reflected image of our absence of color.

What happened to all the gray, or is it grey, in between? Even though we have brilliant, full-color 4K, everything is still black and white. There are only two sides to the story. A pair of binary extremes. Nothing in between and no tolerance for it—if it existed. It's all just too nuanced and complicated to consider looking at the dead channels for answers. Cut and dry, black and white, keep it simple stupid. Those are the solutions that work best. Anything in between is just too prone to fail because it isn't a simple, basic solution or answer to the problem. Nirvana fallacy. Not the conspiracy theory that

Courtney Love had Kurt Cobain killed. It's an informal fallacy but would look good in a sequined tuxedo. It's the current, sad state of affairs. It has to be a perfect plan. Perfect solution fallacy. Assume the perfect solution exists, but doing so is, in itself, a fallacy. Why try if there is any chance of failure? Give up. Watch a YouTube video that simply and plainly shows and tells you what you want to see and hear to ease your worried mind. Accept the "fact" that there is no other way to see it. You can't unsee it. But you (and when I say you, I really mean we) know that everything has been mixed and is now turning gray. Or is it grey?

Static, as an adjective, is defined as lacking in movement, action, or change, especially in a way viewed as undesirable or uninteresting; also concerned with bodies at rest or forces in equilibrium. As a noun, it is noise produced in a radio or television receiver by atmospheric or various natural or manufactured electrical disturbances. Turn your television to an "in-between" channel. Part of the static you'll see is the afterglow of the Big Bang. Once there was only a tiny singularity. Then, all of a sudden, it exploded, and "everything" erupted from it. The blast released enormous amounts of energy and just left it to bounce around. Dead channels of the past are just that, dead and past. We can't see or appreciate the gray now, but it is still out there. It has left the building at the speed of light in every direction. A test pattern, flying blindly through the big nothing of outer space—out into the truest absence of color. Will it be reflected by the biggest black mirror?

Edwin Canfield's book, *Facts, Fictions, and the Forbidden Predictions of the Amazing Criswell!*, is to be released by Headpress Publishing in 2022. It is his first book to be published, but he has a number of projects in the works. From "laid bare" biographies, to the true story of a woman murdered by human wolves, and the real history of the elusive Jackalope. Canfield's main goal and desire as a writer is to take the title of "world's greatest hack" from the late, not-so-great, Leo Guild. Canfield was born in Oklahoma, but currently resides in the desert.
Previous writing credits include:
Filmfax, Spring 2006, "Criswell Predicts: The Life and Prophecies of the Amazing Criswell!"
Find a Death.com, Jeron Charles Criswell King, August 7, 1907 – October 4, 1982, bio
The Zwilight Tone, Fall 2020, "Criswell Returns!"
Connect with Edwin Canfield:
Facebook.com/edwin.canfield
Instagram @forbiddenpredictions

2.

THE SPANIARD

BY

HOWARD GERSHKOWITZ

A Spaniard out of context
no longer consorts with Torquemada.
Minorities were once majorities
but can't remember yesterday's moonlight.

No longer consorting with Torquemada
the angels and the dwarfs beat their razors
but can't remember yesterday's moonlight
or turn the spatula inside out.

The angels and the dwarfs beat their razors
while the high Priestess plays the whore,
turning the spatula inside out
in ecstasy over the frozen wasteland.

While the high Priestess plays the whore
mummies are burned at the stake
in ecstasy over the frozen wasteland
and cities return to the fields.

Mummies are burned at the stake
like a Spaniard out of context
and cities return to the field
where minorities were once majorities.

3.

REDEMPTION

BY

HOWARD GERSHKOWITZ

The aluminum can man
dressed like a leprechaun
slings his black plastic bag
filled with redeemables
over his shoulder,
like Santa Claus in drag.

He fishes through the remains
of yesterday's picnics
in search of metallic recycleum.
Emptied of pop
they pop beneath his heel,
the carbonation long gone.

Pop, pop, pop:
One trash bin, then the next.
More nickels for breakfast
at McDonald's down the street.
Pop, pop, pop.

I wonder
if he's somebody's
Pop.

(Continued on the next page.)

Maybe he took his kids there
for a burger and a cone.
Now he's all alone
in search of other people's residue
of quenched thirsts
to slake his own.

Our eyes meet for a moment.
A silent nod and he's on his way
with the answers to questions
I'd rather not ask.

Howard Gershkowitz is 65, married (42 years) with one child (age 34), and has lived in Arizona since 1981. Maintaining a journal for most of his life, he's accumulated a significant amount of material to write about. To date, he has published a dozen short stories along with a poetry chapbook, *Observations*. His debut novel, *The Operator*, was published in October 2018 by 'All Things That Matter Press.' His latest release, *Not on My Watch*, from the same publisher, is out now and available on Amazon or his website at Gershwriter.com.

Connect with Howard Gershkowitz:
Facebook.com/howard.russell.5682
Instagram @gershwriter1929

4.

A TICKING TIME BOMB IS THE EXACT OPPOSITE OF FREEDOM

BY

CHELSEA HARRINGTON

Tick tock
Goes the clock
So rhythmic
It's almost soothing
Tick tock
Tick tock
It lulls you into a false
Sense of security
Numb from the comfort
Of routine
Tick another night
Tock another morning
Tick another coffee
Tock another dream
But I want to rise
Above the monotony

Don't you know
We regret the failure to act
More than we regret an act
It's hard to grow
From something you didn't do, so
Do something
Do anything

(Continued on next page)

After all, you only get one spin

Before you die,
Make sure you have lived.

5.

THIS ARTICLE ON LIGHT POLLUTION

IS REMINISCENT OF MY POLLUTED THOUGHTS

BY

CHELSEA HARRINGTON

Cities at night burn
Bright under blankets
Of clouds and
In most places
The sky looks as if
It has been emptied
Leaving behind
Vacant spaces
Though a bright shoal of stars
And planets
And galaxies
Gleams above
The city's pale ceiling
Utterly undiminished by the light
We waste
It's still shining
In infinite darkness
We shouldn't pretend

(Continued on next page)

That nothing is lost
We need the night
So we don't lose sight
Of our true place
In the universe.
I'm always struggling
With the feeling
That I don't have enough time.
But what is it
I'm supposed to do next?

6.

What's Glorious and Grotesque

in our Endless Quest for Beauty

by

Chelsea Harrington

The search could be deadly
Girls are literally weighing their self-esteem
Is life not worth living unless you're thin?
Clear, smooth skin?
What about those who are not so symmetrical
Or well-formed?
The technology exists to fabricate
What once we were able to accept
As reliable reflections of reality
And the temptation can be great
To dabble in oxymoronic profundities
Like "subjective truth"

(Continued on next page)

And "artificial reality."
Is anyone immune to feelings of inadequacy?
Eleanor Roosevelt
Was once asked if she had any regrets
"Only one," she said.
She wished she had been prettier.
I will have none of it.
Beauty is not whimsical.
Beauty is truth.
Seek not to alter nature but to celebrate it,
images created
Not as we wish they were
Not as we think they should be
But as they are
Beauty is all the wonderful creative things
that a person is
The question is not
"What is beauty?"
But "By whose definition?"
The most provocative question of all.

Chelsea Harrington was born and raised in Leavenworth, Kansas, though she has called Lawrence home since 2019. Chelsea currently works as a full-time therapist but has always had a passion for the arts and incorporates creativity in her personal and professional life in any way she can, including assisting with starting and taking on the role of Associate Director of LV Arts, an arts-based nonprofit organization in her hometown.

For the entirety of her life, Chelsea has been creating in some capacity. Starting in early childhood, Chelsea would write and send short poems to "Highlights" magazine, and though every poem was rejected, she persevered and built up her artistic skills by engaging in community art classes in calligraphy, creative writing, pottery, drawing, and painting. Chelsea began entering (and finally winning!) art and writing contests in elementary and middle school, leading to workshops in playwriting with the Coterie Theatre at Crown Center at 14, painting two murals at the historic Riverfront Community Center in Leavenworth at 17, and creating and selling her own books of collage poetry. Chelsea is very involved in the poetry community in Lawrence and Leavenworth and regularly participates in open mic opportunities. She also creates cutout and collage-style art and poetry pieces that she shares over social media.

While Chelsea has had photographs of artwork published, she is pleased to announce this is her first publication of poetry. "Highlights" magazine missed their chance.

Connect with Chelsea Harrington:
Facebook.com/Chelsea.harrington.art
Instagram: @ccharrington90

7.

RAYANNE

BY

MICHAEL MAYES

Tommy Thompson was lost. He had turned onto Rodair Road nearly an hour ago and should have reached the Spurlock turnoff long before now. *Shortcut my ass*, he thought. Tommy was already fighting his guilt for leaving his grandfather alone tonight. He didn't need any more complications. It was the first New Year's Eve since his grandmother had died. He had offered to stay home, but Gramps insisted that he go to Tess's party and have fun. "You're only young once," he said as he tossed Tommy the keys to his grandmother's Toyota Camry. Now, however, it was looking more and more like he'd left his grandfather alone for nothing. On top of the guilt, he was angry—angry that he would be late to Tess's party. He'd been laying the groundwork with Tess for three months now, and tonight was going to be the night, he was sure of it. Being over an hour late, however, was not going to help his chances. Worse, that douchebag, Tim Simon, was going to be at the party. Tim had been eyeballing Tess even longer than he had. The difference was that Tommy actually liked Tess, maybe even loved her. Tim was only after one thing and was usually very adept at getting it. The thought of Tim moving in on Tess made Tommy nauseous. "Damn it!" he said, hitting the wheel with his fist. "Where the hell am I?"

The familiar blacktop of Rodair Road had played out at some point while Tommy was torturing himself with thoughts of losing Tess. He was now driving on a rough caliche road that badly needed grading. "No, no, no, this isn't right," he said. Tommy had driven down Rodair Road dozens of times since he had been seeing Tess, and this was not Rodair Road.

Rodair Road was twenty miles of gun barrel-straight blacktop that cut through the marshy Hilldebrandt Bayou, connecting Highway 365 with Spurlock Road. There were no curves or side roads. There simply was no way a person could get turned around while driving it, yet somehow, he had managed to get lost anyway. He shook his head and thought, *Tommy, my boy, you could screw up a wet dream.*

Distracted by the act of mentally berating himself, Tommy failed to see a deep rut in the road and drove right into it without braking. He heard a sickening crunch. The car shuddered violently and pitched to the right, slamming his head into the driver's side window. He hit the brakes and brought the vehicle to a stop in the middle of the road, whatever road it was. "Damn it!" Tommy said, rubbing his left temple. "That was definitely not good."

Once the cobwebs cleared, Tommy stepped out of his vehicle to inspect the damage. That crunching he had heard sounded bad, like, *expensive* bad. He circled the Camry and, to his surprise, found no cosmetic damage. He did, however, note that he had blown out his left front tire. He could hear the air hissing as it escaped its steel-belted, vulcanized prison. Tommy sighed in resignation. While it could have been worse, there was no way he would make it to Tess's party now. He pulled his phone from his pocket and dialed his grandfather's number. *This is going to be a fun conversation,* he thought. As it turned out, he shouldn't have worried. The phone was dead. *I just charged it! This doesn't make any sense!* he thought.

Tommy flung the now useless device into the backseat and leaned up against the crippled Camry. He looked up and down the unfamiliar road but could not see far as it was amazingly dark. No streetlights—no other traffic. Even the moon was blocked by the tall cypress and tupelo trees that loomed just beyond the narrow bar ditches lining both sides of the road. For the first time, Tommy realized how alone and lost he really was. "I need to get out of here," he said aloud to himself, walking to the back of the vehicle to grab the jack and spare tire from the trunk. He was not confident the donut-sized spare could handle this rough road, but there was simply no other option. As he came around the car with the tire and jack, he saw her. Not thirty feet in front of the car, there was a girl.

Tommy's knees buckled, and he nearly fell due to the shock of her appearing out of nowhere. "Holy shit, you scared me!" he said. The girl said nothing, nor did she move. Tommy tentatively walked around the car and took several cautious steps toward her. "Hey, I'm sorry," he said. "I was just startled. It's really creepy out here, and you're the first person I've seen." The girl did not answer. Instead, she just stared at Tommy in a way that made him uncomfortable. *She's looking at me like I'm something good to eat*, he thought, but immediately dismissed the notion as ridiculous. It was only then that he noticed the girl's attire. She was wearing a white button-down shirt with the sleeves rolled up to her elbows. The shirt was tucked into a dark knee-length skirt with what looked like a pink poodle embroidered on it. Below the skirt, she wore short socks and white and black leather shoes. "Are those golf shoes?" Tommy asked himself. The girl's blonde hair was pulled back in a ponytail with a sheer pink scarf tied around it. She was beautiful, somehow radiant, standing there at the edge of the reach of the headlights.

Tommy took a slow step forward. "My name is Tommy," he said. "Please, don't be afraid."

"I'm not afraid," the girl replied.

The sound of her voice startled Tommy, and he jumped like he'd been goosed with a cattle prod. She's right, he thought, *I'm the only scared one out here.*

"Good, that's…good," he stammered. "I, uh, I had a little car trouble."

"So, I see," she said.

Tommy blushed. He was glad it was dark—maybe she wouldn't notice. "What about you?" he asked. "What are you doing out here all alone?"

She furrowed her brow, and her face took on an angry expression. Her voice, however, was calm and measured when she replied, "You ask a lot of questions...Tommy."

Tommy felt the blood rushing to his cheeks for a second time. "Oh, hey...I'm sorry. I'm not trying to be nosey or anything," he said. "It's just that this is not the sort of place I would expect to run into a pretty girl in the middle of the night."

The girl's face softened. She cocked her head slightly and asked, "You think I'm pretty?"

Tommy's face was now so hot he was sure the girl would be able to feel the heat radiating off of it even at a distance. "Uh, well, yeah," he said. "I do."

She smiled for the first time and stepped toward him. She looked past him at the jack and spare and asked, "What are those for?"

"Huh? Oh, those," he said. "I have a flat and need to change the tire."

"It doesn't look flat to me," she said.

Tommy turned and looked down at the left front tire. It appeared fully inflated and in perfect condition. *What the hell?* he thought. *How can that be?*

"I don't understand," he said. "It was flat as a pancake not five minutes ago."

"Well, it seems fine now," she said.

As she stepped closer to him, Tommy caught her scent. She

smelled wonderful.

"Would you mind giving me a ride?"

Tommy just stared at her. *God, she's gorgeous.* She turned her head slightly and widened her eyes in a *Well?* expression that snapped him back to reality.

"A ride? Um, yeah, sure," he finally managed to get out. "Of course."

She smiled, said, "Thank you," and walked to the passenger side of the Camry. She stopped before opening the door, turned to look at him, and said, "My name is Rayanne."

#

They had been driving for ten minutes without a word passing between them. Each time Tommy glanced over, which was never for more than a second at a time as the road was steadily growing more treacherous and required his full attention, she merely stared straight ahead. It was almost as if she had forgotten he was there at all.

"Should I turn on the radio?" Tommy finally worked up the nerve to ask.

She turned, gave him a smile that caused his heart to race, and said, "Yes, I would like that."

"Great," he said. He clicked the radio on, but instead of music, there was only static. He turned the dial from one end to the other to find a station but had no luck. Only an obnoxious crackling sound rewarded his efforts. "Maybe something got disconnected when I hit that rut," Tommy said. "Sorry about that."

A slight smile crossed Rayanne's lips, and she said, "Let me give it a try."

She studied the console for a few moments before reaching

out and turning the radio dial. Almost immediately, the sound of Ritchie Valens singing "La Bamba" filled the car. Rayanne smiled and said, "There, that's better." She seemed very pleased with herself.

"How the heck did you do that?" Tommy asked.

"Do what?" she replied.

"Find a radio station," he said. "I tried from one end of the dial to the other and got nothing."

Rayanne, once again staring straight ahead, said, "Just lucky, I guess."

"La Bamba" was followed by a pre-jumpsuit-wearing Elvis Presley crooning "Love Me Tender." *Weird*, Tommy thought. *I didn't know we got an oldies station in Pine Island.* "What station is this?" he asked Rayanne.

"K-95, of course!" she replied. "They play all the best songs."

More puzzled than ever, Tommy said, "Never heard of it." He then suggested, "Maybe you could find a station that plays something newer?"

Rayanne turned to face him and gave him a smile that did not quite reach her eyes. "Newer? You're silly, Tommy."

"Maybe I am," he mumbled and decided to change the subject. "So, you never did tell me how you got way out here in the middle of nowhere."

The cross-expression Tommy had seen on her face earlier when he had broached the subject returned. She once again turned to face straight ahead and crossed her arms in the manner of a petulant child. "If you must know," she said, "I was left out here."

"Left?" he asked. "Who left you?"

15

Tommy turned and looked at Rayanne. Though he was seeing her only in profile, he could tell her bottom lip was quivering. He then saw a single tear escape her left eye and run down her cheek. "Barry did," she said. "My boyfriend, Barry."

"Some boyfriend," Tommy said so quietly it was barely audible.

"Well, he's not my boyfriend anymore," Rayanne said. "He said he wanted to take me out to look at the stars before we went to the dance, but he didn't want to look at the stars. That isn't what he wanted to do at all."

Tommy, feeling guilty for having asked the question, felt his stomach tighten into a knot. "Hey, I'm sorry, you don't have to talk about it if you don't want to."

"He got fresh," she said as if she had not heard him. "*Really* fresh. When I said 'no,' he got very angry. He said that I might as well let him do what he wanted because he was going to tell everybody at school that's what happened anyway."

Fresh? Tommy thought to himself. The feeling something was wrong hung in the air like a dense fog.

Rayanne spun in her seat to look at him, her face streaked with tears. "Oh, Tommy, what am I going to do? My reputation will be ruined!"

Tommy pulled the car over and tentatively put his arm around the now nearly hysterical girl. "It's going to be okay, don't worry. I know guys like Barry," he said. "Everybody knows they're full of shit."

She looked up at him and asked, "Are you sure?"

"I am," he replied.

Rayanne summoned a weak smile, leaned in closer to him, and whispered, "You shouldn't use such language, Tommy, but thank you." She kissed him lightly on the cheek. Her lips were shockingly cold.

"You're welcome," Tommy replied as a wave of exhilaration washed over him. "So, should I take you home?"

Rayanne scrunched up her nose. "Oh, no, not home. I'm supposed to be at the New Year's Eve dance. If I come home early, my daddy will want to know why," she said.

"Maybe he should know," he suggested.

"Oh, Tommy, no, that would *not* be good. I think Daddy would kill Barry if he found out what he did."

"Okay then, where do you want to go?"

After pondering the question for a few moments, Rayanne's face lit up like a Broadway night. "The dance!" she said. "You can take me to the dance!"

"Well, I'd feel kind of funny just dropping you off somewhere," Tommy said. "Will there be anyone there to take you home?"

"I didn't mean for you to just drop me off, silly," she replied. "I want you to be my date."

Tommy thought of Tess and hesitated. Rayanne seemed to sense the nature of his thoughts, and her face darkened. "You won't leave me too, will you, Tommy?"

A feeling unlike any he had ever felt before came over Tommy at that moment. It was as if every cell in his body was telling him to run. The hairs on the back of his neck stiffened. Then, as suddenly as it had appeared, the feeling was gone. "No, no, of course not," he said. "It's just that I'm not really dressed to go to a dance."

The darkness did not leave Rayanne's face for several moments. It was as if she were considering his words to see if they had the weight of truth in them. Finally, her face softened, and she broke into a smile. "Good!" she said. "Don't worry about your clothes. It's just a sock hop. It isn't like it's the prom or something."

"Oh, that explains it," Tommy said.

A puzzled look crossed Rayanne's face. "Explains what?"

"The way you're dressed," he said. "You know, like it's the fifties."

She looked at Tommy with a blank expression that lasted just long enough to become awkward. Finally, her smile returned. "You really are a strange boy, aren't you, Tommy?"

Feeling a bit bewildered, Tommy decided to treat her question as one of the rhetorical variety and changed the subject. "Where is this dance?"

"At the ELK's Lodge," she said. "It isn't too much farther. This is going to be so much fun. I *love* to dance."

"The ELK's Lodge?" he asked. "Are you sure? There's no lodge or anything else on Rodair Road."

"Really, Tommy?" Rayanne said in a tone that made it very clear she was not amused. "If you don't stop teasing me, I am going to dance with other boys."

Who talks like that? he wondered.

Before his mind could get too far down that path, Rayanne pointed ahead and practically squealed, "There it is!"

Tommy looked down the road and could make out the glow of a security light. As he drove closer, he could see a sign that read "ELK's Lodge #144, Established 1934." *Where am I?* he thought as he drove into the unpaved parking lot.

#

Tommy found a spot at the far end of the parking area. Rayanne barely waited for the Camry to come to a stop before she hopped out. He threw the car in park, shoved the now-familiar uneasy feeling that something was not right back from whence it had come, and stepped out into the night. The building that housed ELKS Lodge #144 was pristine white and seemed to almost glow despite the pitch blackness of the surrounding marsh and forest. Tommy could hear the sound of The Champs playing "Tequila" blasting from inside the dance hall, even from the back of the lot.

"Hey, I know that song," he said.

"Tommy," Rayanne replied, "everyone knows that song. Come on!"

The blonde beauty took his hand and began to lead him toward the building. Her hand was frigid.

"Are you cold?" he asked. "You can wear my jacket if you want."

"No, I'm fine," she said. "Besides, I don't think I've known you long enough to wear your jacket. What would people say?"

For the second time that evening, Tommy wondered, *Who talks like that?*

"Oh, no," Rayanne said.

Tommy turned to look at her and asked, "What is it?"

She pointed at a red and white vehicle. "That's Barry's car."

Tommy gazed at the sparkling vehicle with admiration. It was a 1957 Chevrolet Bel Air, and it looked to be in perfect condition. "Wow," Tommy whispered. "That's a beauty."

"Hmmph," Rayanne grunted.

For the first time since pulling into the parking area, Tommy took note of the other vehicles in the lot. They were all vintage and in impeccable shape. "Man, you guys really went all out with the fifties theme, didn't you?" he said.

Rayanne said nothing. She only frowned and crossed her arms to indicate her impatience with him. Tommy failed to notice. He was enthralled with the assortment of classic cars and trucks present. "There's a '58 Thunderbird," he said. "And there's a '59 Corvette." He turned, and to his wonder, saw a '53 Plymouth Suburban parked next to a '57 Chevy 3200 pick-up.

"Can we go in, please?" Rayanne pleaded.

"One second," Tommy said. "See that truck right there?"

"Yes."

"That's a 1956 Ford F100. My grandfather had one just like it when he was in high school. I've seen pictures of it in his old photo album. This is the first one I've ever seen in person."

Rayanne said nothing. She only looked longingly at the door of the lodge.

"I wish he were here to see this one," Tommy said.

"Can we *please* go in now?" Rayanne asked. "They're playing Santo and Johnny."

The sound of "Sleep Walk" reached Tommy's ears. "I know this one, too," he said. "Gramps plays it now and then, usually when he's missing Grandma."

"That's nice," Rayanne said as she took his hand again.

Tommy took one more look at the old yet somehow perfectly new, '56 Ford truck, then allowed himself to be pulled up the three steps leading to the front doors of the strangely incandescent ELKS Lodge. The two entered just as the first notes of Little Anthony's "Tears on My Pillow" began to play.

#

Rayanne led Tommy into a long room with a hardwood floor.

At the far end of the hall, there was a D.J. with some seriously out-dated equipment. Above the D.J., a banner read *"Welcome 1960!"* The words gently rippled as air stirred from the various ceiling fans vainly attempting to cool the room.

1960? he thought, but his questions left his mind when the temperature of the room hit him. It was like being inside a pizza oven. "Damn, it's hot in here," he said.

Rayanne did not seem to hear. She only stared, mesmerized by the swaying couples who crowded the dance floor, an odd glimmer in her eye.

Against the left wall of the room stood a refreshment table. On it, dozens of paper napkins provided a resting place for exactly two Oreos. In the center of the table sat a huge punch bowl. Upon seeing it, Tommy realized he was burning with thirst. "I'm going to get some punch," he said. "Would you like some?"

"No, thank you," Rayanne replied. "I just want to dance."

"I'll hurry," he said.

Suddenly, a concerned look fell upon Rayanne's face, and she said, "Be careful. Barry said he was going to spike the punch." She looked left and then right before adding, "If he did, it would be positively scandalous."

Tommy, thinking he could probably use a drink, said, "I'll be careful," and continued toward the refreshment table.

Once at the table, he grabbed a pre-filled Dixie cup and slammed the punch in one gulp. It was not spiked. *Too bad*, he thought, grabbing another cup. He couldn't remember ever being this thirsty.

He threw the two paper cups into a trash can and turned to look for Rayanne. As he scanned the room, he was startled by the realization that he seemed to be able to see through the couples who were now moving slowly to the tune of "Let It Be Me." Tommy closed his eyes tightly, shook his head, and thought, *Maybe that punch was spiked after all.* When he opened his eyes, the couples appeared solid enough, but the feeling that all was not as it should be was stronger. This time, the feeling refused to be pushed aside. *No one is talking,* he thought. *Nobody is speaking.* There was the sound of the music and nothing else.

Rayanne reappeared at his side, causing him to start. "What's wrong, Tommy?"

"I'm not sure," he said in a low voice. "Why isn't anyone talking?"

It seemed he had, once again, asked the wrong question as her face flushed with anger. "Because it is a dance, not a debate club meeting," she said through gritted teeth. "Now, are you going to dance with me or not?"

Not waiting for an answer, she grabbed Tommy by the arm and tugged him out to the center of the dance floor. He could vaguely make out the sound of The Platters singing "Smoke Gets in Your Eyes." *Did we just walk through that couple?* he wondered. *That can't be. Why is it so hard to think—to breathe?*

"Rayanne," he croaked. "I'm not feeling very well."

She looked at him with the same odd expression she was wearing when he first saw her standing in the road. "Shh," she whispered. "It's all going to be alright, Tommy. It will be over soon."

Over? What was she talking about? "Rayanne, it's just so hot in here. I can't breathe." He felt he was on the verge of collapsing.

"I know, I know," she said softly, taking his face in her hands. Heaven itself could not have felt better than her icy touch at that moment. "There, that's better, isn't it?" she asked. "It won't be long now."

What won't be long? he wanted to ask but couldn't form the words. He was having a hard time seeing her now, though they were only inches apart. It was as if he was seeing her through a haze. *No,* his mind screamed, *not haze...smoke!*

With all the strength he had left, Tommy lifted his head and looked around the room. The other couples were gone, and an orange glow filled the building. He became conscious of the heat and could feel his skin blistering. Black smoke stung his eyes and filled his lungs. He choked on the scorching air and felt his insides burning. As he looked down at Rayanne, her eyes were as red as the flames that had now fully engulfed the building.

"You aren't going to leave me, are you, Tommy?" she hissed.

Rayanne's body was now almost fully transparent. Through her body, Tommy watched one of the windows on the far side of the room explode.

"Rayanne, no!" he screamed. "We've got to go, now!"

Completely spectral in appearance, she gripped him with frightening strength and pulled him close to her. "You promised, Tommy," she said. "You promised you would dance with me."

Without warning, a new voice, a male voice, was in his ear, "Let's go! This place is about to come down!" Tommy felt a new pair of hands on his shoulders, trying to pull him toward the door.

Rayanne, would not relinquish her grip, and Tommy did not budge.

"Jesus, buddy!" the unseen man behind him screamed. "We've got to go, now!"

Tommy could feel himself swooning and knew he would die here if he did not do something. He summoned the last of his strength, reached up behind Rayanne and jerked her backward by her ponytail. That was the slight break his savior needed. He felt himself being wrenched from her grip and dragged across the hardwood floor by his collar.

"Noooo!" she howled. "Noooo!"

He watched as Rayanne slowly faded from view. He could not tell if the smoke was obscuring her or if she was melting back into the oblivion from which she had risen. The last thing Tommy saw was her burning red eyes, and then, there was nothing.

#

The jostling of paramedics placing him on a stretcher stirred Tommy from his stupor. Upon awakening, he attempted to get smoke-free air into his oxygen-starved lungs by inhaling deeply. He regretted it immediately as a searing pain filled his chest. He coughed, gagged, and unceremoniously threw up all over himself. "Easy fella," one of the first responders said. "You're going to be okay." His head throbbed to the rhythm of the pulsing emergency flashers as he tried desperately to cling to consciousness—afraid if things went dark, he would never again see the light of day, but he could feel himself slipping away again. Tommy only barely felt the paramedic place the oxygen mask onto his face before the sensation of being lifted and moved made him reel. Just before he was loaded into the ambulance, he turned his head in time to see Rayanne. She was standing in front of his Camry, only thirty feet away. He felt his mind come unhinged, and the blackness returned.

#

Three days later, with the help of his grandfather, Tommy walked into the house they shared. As the two stepped through the door, he became light-headed and started to buckle. The old man grabbed him by the arms and prevented him from taking a nasty fall. For just a moment, panic seized Tommy's soul—he had felt such a grip before. The moment quickly passed as he looked at his grandfather's face and realized the grip he felt on this day was warm and not deathly cold. *He's still so strong*, he thought.

Sensing Tommy's thoughts, the old man said, "I guess chopping my own wood all these years has finally come in handy."

Once inside, his grandfather helped Tommy to the couch. The older man took a seat in his ancient recliner, opposite his grandson. Tommy could tell his grandfather was deeply troubled. With a hoarse voice, he asked, "What's on your mind, Gramps?"

For a moment, the old man seemed to wrestle with whether or not he wanted to say anything. Finally, a resigned expression settled on his face, and he said, "I've been thinking a lot about that story you told me."

"Gramps, I know it's crazy, but I swear it's all true." He felt like crying.

"Mmm-hmm," the old man grunted. "I think there is something you should know."

Tommy said nothing, but his eyes asked the questions for him.

"You know I graduated from Pine Island High School in 1960?"

Tommy nodded.

"Technically, my senior year was the 1959-60 school year."

Tommy remained silent and watched his grandfather struggle to come up with the words to continue. Finally, the old man sighed deeply and said, "There was even less to Pine Island then than there is now. Lots of the roads that are paved or black-topped now were just dirt roads back then."

"I know, Gramps," Tommy said.

The old man held up a hand. "Let me finish before I change my mind. One of those roads that were just dirt and clay was Rodair

Road."

Tommy swallowed hard, and a shiver ran through his entire body. "Yeah, so?"

"So," the old man said, "as you know, there is nothing on Rodair Road these days. It's just swamp and woods out there now—"

Tommy's eyes widened. Surely this story was not going where he feared it was.

His grandfather went on, "—but there used to be a building out that way. From what I was told, it was built in the twenties or early thirties during prohibition. It was a speakeasy."

"A speakeasy?" Tommy asked.

The old man nodded, "That's right, they sold shine— homemade whiskey there. Nobody much cared. It was way out in the middle of the woods. My daddy told me even the sheriff stopped in to have a nip from time to time. As long as the booze was kept out of town, he left the moonshiners alone."

"Why are you telling me this?" Tommy whispered.

"Bear with me, son," he replied. "Once prohibition ended, the place was sold to a group called the Benevolent and Protective Order of Elks."

Tommy could feel the blood leave his face. "Oh, my God, it became an ELKS Lodge."

The old man nodded. "The ELKS did a lot of good work back then—fed and housed a lot of folks that didn't have a pot to pee in. Those were hard days. The Great Depression was at its worst in the mid-to-late thirties. Daddy told me that he and his brothers might've starved if it hadn't been for the ELKS."

Tommy felt a cold fear deep in his soul. "What else?"

The old man continued, "The Lodge also served as a community center for Pine Island. It was a place where the Ladies Auxiliary or Boy Scouts could meet. All kinds of organizations met there or rented it out, including Pine Island High School."

"For dances," Tommy whispered in a trembling voice.

"Yes," the old man said, "for dances."

Tommy stiffened. "Gramps, I don't think I want to hear anymore. I—"

The old man cut him off. "No, you have to hear. You have to know, not only that I believe your story, but *why* I believe it."

The earnestness in his grandfather's voice made Tommy realize the old man *needed* to share this tale. How long it had been festering deep in his heart, Tommy could only wonder. "Okay, Gramps," he said.

"Good, that's good," the old man said. "The school rented that lodge out for lots of dances, including one on January 31, 1959."

"New Year's Eve."

"That's right, New Year's Eve," his grandfather said. "That was some night, let me tell you. I think the only time I ever saw your grandmother look prettier was the day we got married."

You were there, Tommy thought.

"It was a fine night, yes sir, a fine night," the old man continued, "until just a few minutes before midnight."

That was your truck.

"That's when some idiot—"

You were there.

"—decided to toss a half-smoked Chesterfield into a wastebasket."

"The fire," Tommy said.

"Yes," his grandfather said. "That's how the fire started."

Tommy sat and stared straight ahead, seeing nothing but the image of the burning lodge in his mind's eye.

"That place was a tinderbox," the old man said. "It was completely engulfed in minutes." Tommy's grandfather stood up and walked over to an antique desk. He pulled open a drawer that, by the sound of it, had not been opened in a long time, and the old man removed a bottle of scotch. With trembling hands, he poured a glass and drank it down in one gulp. "There, that's better," he said.

"Gramps, this…this is impossible," Tommy said.

The old man nodded, "But it's true just the same." He leaned down and looked into Tommy's eyes. "You know it's true. You can feel it."

Tommy gave only a barely perceptible nod.

"Like I said, the lodge became an inferno," he continued. "Even so, everyone got out. At least that's what we thought."

Not everyone.

"We were all in the parking lot watching the place burn when a guy named Barry Hunt came running up to me and said, 'My girlfriend is still in there! You gotta help her!'" The old man paused and walked back toward the ancient desk.

"Barry," Tommy parroted.

With his back to Tommy, the grandfather continued, "It never dawned on me to wonder why Barry didn't go in after her himself. I just knew I had to try and help. Your grandmother tried to stop me, but I shook her off and ran back inside."

Tommy watched his grandfather poured a second glass of scotch. After taking a sip, he said, "I don't know what hell is like, son, and I pray I never find out, but the inside of that lodge had to have been close. The roof was falling in, windows were exploding, and the heat… it was awful." After steeling himself with another sip of alcohol, he continued, "I didn't see a girl, but right in the middle of the room stood one guy. I didn't recognize him—something I wondered a lot about over the years since Pine Island was such a small place, but I ran over to him and said—"

"Let's go. This place is about to come down," Tommy said softly.

The old man nodded. "It was the strangest thing. The guy just stood there like he was in some kind of trance. I tried to grab him, but, for some reason, I couldn't move him an inch. I'm ashamed to admit it, but I almost left him there. I figured if he wanted to kill himself, that was his right, but I didn't have to go with him."

Tommy suddenly felt a familiar cold sensation on his skin. He could not have spoken at that moment, even if he had wanted to. He was frozen in fear.

"I started to leave but didn't even take one step before I turned back around," his grandfather said. "Something came over me, and I just knew I had to get this guy out of there. I grabbed him by the collar of his jacket and pulled. I think he passed out at the same time because he just fell over backward. That was fine with me. It made it easier to drag him across the floor and out of there."

Tommy mouthed the words, "What happened then?" but could not be sure if he had managed to create any sound. Even so, his grandfather seemed to understand the question.

"I dragged him out to the parking area near my truck," the old man said. "The entire building collapsed not ten seconds after I had him out. It was a close call."

Tommy watched his grandfather walk back to the antique desk, where he opened the same squeaky drawer. This time he removed what looked like one of his photo albums.

"It was about then we heard the sirens. The fire department, such as it was back then, was on its way," the old man said. "Everyone had turned to look down the road at the approaching fire engine when the fella I pulled out of the building coughed. I knelt down to see if he was okay, and he looked up at me and said, 'Thank you.' Then…"

The old man hesitated and began trembling uncontrollably.

"Gramps, are you alright? Gramps?"

The old man took a deep breath. "The first fire truck wheeled into the lot about that time, and I turned to watch it pull in," he said. "When I looked back, that fella was gone." His grandfather turned and leaned in close enough for Tommy to smell the scotch on his breath. "As God as my witness, he was just…gone."

Tommy said nothing. He just sat, mouth agape, struggling to process what he had been told.

"It turned out Barry was right. His girlfriend, Rayanne Hebert, never made it out," the old man said. "The firemen said she probably died from smoke inhalation before the building came down on her, but I'm not so sure. I thought I heard screams."

They sat in silence for several minutes. Finally, the old man spoke again. "I've wondered what happened to that fella ever since that night. Now, I guess I know."

The old man handed Tommy the photo album he had removed from the creaky desk drawer moments before. Tommy opened it and saw an article from the *East Texas Sentinel* dated January 1, 1960, pasted to the first page. The headline read, "Pine Island ELKS Lodge destroyed – Inferno takes the life of high school senior." A grainy black-and-white photo accompanied the article. Among the throng of stupefied teenagers in their fifties-era clothing was one young man whose appearance was quite different. He wore a PIHS letter jacket, but his jeans were not rolled up and looked lighter than those worn by the other boys. He was also wearing a pair of Nike cross-trainers. *It's impossible*, he thought.

"Here," his grandfather said as he handed him a magnifying glass. "Look closer."

Shaking badly, Tommy leaned in and examined the oddly dressed figure in the photo. Staring back at him, through the magnifying glass and across a gulf of more than sixty years, was his own face.

The End

Michael Mayes is a teacher of history and former coach who resides in Central Texas. An avid folklorist, he has long been fascinated by the ghostly tales of historical and contemporary Texas as well as mysteries of the natural world. Mayes has authored two books, *Patty: A Sasquatch Story* and *Shadow Cats: The Black Panthers of North America*, and is the owner/writer of the *Texas Cryptid Hunter* blog. Michael can be reached via email at Mikemayes44@yahoo.com or via his website at Michaelcmayes.com.

8.

THE BRIAR ROSE SYNDROME

BY

JOSEPH D. NEWCOMER

Jan. 20, 1999

Hello. My name is Dexter Nurse, and I have fifty-five minutes to live. Yesterday, I decided to write an email of my last moments so that it might help someone like me and Phillipe, that poor bastard. Last month, I went to a psychiatrist because I have been sleeping for one minute more each night for the past four or five years. At first, it wasn't a problem because I'm a writer, and being awake for only six hours a day didn't really interfere with work. It did interfere with some other things. My fiancé dumped me, and all of my plants died. (Let me take twelve seconds to apologize for grammar and punctuation, for I only have a short time and don't want to waste it on editing typos. This is what first drafts look like. It will be as riddled with errors as my brain.) Two years ago, when I was down to about six hours, it was suggested that I go to the doctor. Well, actually, she told me to "Get some fucking help!" So, I went. After Twenty eight hours, fifty-two minutes, and twelve different tests, the doctors were still baffled and did what doctors do when they have no idea what's wrong. They gave me sixteen different drugs and vitamins. I took them for a whole year. Nothing helped, and every couple of weeks, I had to drop five or six pills because their schedules no longer fit into my waking hours. After that, I took speed, which made me feel more awake, but I didn't sleep any less. Then I took cocaine, and all that did was take more of my time because every night when I had about five minutes left, I'd do as many

lines as I could, and when I woke up, I'd have to clean the blood
Jan. 21, 1999

-off of myself from the nose bleeds. Sorry, I set myself up at my computer so that when I woke up a minute later today, I could just keep writing. Anyway, coke didn't work, so I thought about how if you take Ritalin and you're not hyperactive, it works as a stimulant, and I took some downers. I'm not sure what they were, but they were blue. I got them from a person I went to college with. He was a drug addict studying to be a pharmacist. He told me to take two on a full stomach with a glass of water. When I told him how much coke I did, he told me to take ten with a fifth of Jake Daniels. But they only made me sleep through the three hours and twenty-six minutes I was supposed to be awake--scared the shit out of me too. Every night I fall asleep at twelve. I felt myself nodding off, so I looked at the clock, and it was exactly ten minutes after I took them. Then I passed out and woke up the next day, one minute after I had the previous day. Needless to say, I stopped taking drugs. I was a junkie for a year and a half. All right, so last month I went to a psychiatristtt.9.8777 ......9t9999999bbbbbbbbbbhhh   999999....
99999999999998888888888766666666677777777787999999999bb
bbbbbbbbbbbbbbbbbbbbbbbbbbbbbbbbbbbbbbbbbbbbbbbbbbbbbbbbbb
bbbbbbbbbbbbbbbbbbbbbbbbbbbbbbbbbbbbbbbbbbbbbbbbbbbbbbbbbb
bbbbbbbbbbbbbbbbbbbbbbbbbbbbbbbbbbbbbbbbbbbbbbbbbbbbbbbbbb
bbbbbbbbbbbbbbbbbbbbbbbbbbbbbbbbbbbbbbbbbbbbbbbbbbbbbbbbbb
bbbbbbbbbbbbbbbbbbbbbbbbbbbbbbbbbbbbbbbbbbbbbbbbbbbbbbbbbb
bbbbbbbbbbbbbbbbbbbbbbbbbbbbbbbbbbbbbbbbbbbbbbbbbbbbbbbbbb
bbbbbbbbbbbbbbbbbbbbbbbbbbbbbbbb7iiiii8vllh7bhhhggggggvhvvv
vvvvvbbbbbbbbbbbbbbbbbbbbbbbbbbbbbbbbbbbbbbbbbhbbbbbbbbbbhbhhv
gggggggggggggg-
bbbbbbbbbbbbbbbbvvvvvvvvvgggggggggggggghggggggggg8ll8gbbbbbbb
bbbbbbbbbbbbbbbbbbbbbbbbbbbbbbbbbbbbbbbbbbbbbbbbbbbbbbbbbb
bbbbbbbbbbbbbbbbbbbbbbbbbbbbbbbbbbbbbbbbbbbbbbbbbbbbbbbbbb

bbbbbbbbbbbbbbbbbbbbbbbbbbbbbbbbbbb7g7777777777777hhhhgvbbb
biiiiiiiiiiiiiiiiiiiiiiiiiiiiiiiiiivvvvvvvvggggggggggg8ybnyiiny8iyybbbbbbb
bbbbbbbbbbbbbbbbbbb   Bbbbbbbbbbbbbbbbbbbbbbbb
Bbbbbbbbbbbbbbbbbbbbbbbbbbbbbbbbbbbbbbbbbbbbbbbbbbbbbbbbyou are
a moron! Next time you may want to move your laptop before you
start drooling on it. I took the last of my things and some things of
yours that I wanted because "you're dying," and I can see why with
all of the coke everywhere. I hope you straighten out, but I can't be
part of it. I loved you. Goodbye Dexter.

-Julie

Jan. 22, 1999

Isn't she a sweetheart? Good thing she came or you would
have been looking at page after page of B's. I deleted about four
pages of them, but last night when I fell asleep, I spilled a moldy
glass of orange juice on my mouse touchpad, and it seems moldy orange juice isn't very good for mouse touchpads, so I had to use my
backspace key, and I decided it was taking too long. It took so long
for me to go to the psychiatrist because I hate it when someone who
doesn't know me tries to help me. That's also why it took so long for
me to go to the hospital and a shit load of good that did! I told him
what was going on, and he listened, but it was obvious that he didn't
believe a word of it. After my forty-five minutes of allocated conscious state, I fell asleep in his chair, mid-sentence. After days under
his observation, he believed me. He said he'd done everything he
could do to wake me up, splashing water on my face, slapping me,
smelling salts. All of which he should have realized wasn't going to
work after I told him about the drugs, but still, he felt compelled to
try. Then he did one night of internet research and found out that one
other person had gone through the same thing I was. I did a little in-

ternet research myself, but after seeing that I probably had one of any number of terminal illnesses, I got a little discouraged and went back to the coke. Anyway, the other guy's name was Phillipe Esillo. He was a Spanish bartender. Dr. Hallow let me read the last part of his file. His wife took his kids and left. He lost his job, and then he killed himself. He wired four gallon jugs of tequila to the ceiling above his bed. He hooked them all up to a tube, and shoved it down his throat. With three minutes left, or in my time, the last two days of his life, he was going to drink himself to death in his sleep. But right after he fell asleep, the four bottles fell on his head and crushed his skull he never got to see his last minu

Jan. 23 1999

Dr. Hallow diagnosed me with what they diagnosed Phillipe, that poor bastard, with. "An acute, novel mental psychosis due to controlled, narcoleptic hypersomnia, resulting in an undeterminable subconscious or catatonic state and possibly death" or as Dr. Hallow decided to name it, "Briar Rose Syndrome." That prick was excited because he got to name it. Apparently, Sleeping Beauty Syndrome was already taken, and while the symptoms were not entirely dissimilar, Briar Rose was much more severe and unique enough to call it something of its own. No one had named it when Phillipe had it, kind of fucked up if you ask me. Why "Briar Rose" you probably weren't wondering, and I won't be around to answer if anyone ever does? It was Sleeping Beauty's original name or some shit. Hallow googled it. He said he thought it was brought on by stress, chronic boredom, and a paralyzing fear of death. I don't know anyone who doesn't have at least two of the three. I kept going back after the diagnosis, but Dr. Hallow could find no reason for my and that poor bastard Phillipe's problem. He said that there were no histories of illness or abuse in both cases, except for the alcohol poor Phillipe tried to drink at the very end and the speed, coke, and downers I took, of course. And after a couple of weeks, it just took too long to get there. I fell asleep twice on the subway. That's not the healthiest thing to do. Petula Clark, that's damn good advice. From what I could tell, I was pissed on, someone tattooed a naked woman on my arm, and my shoes, jacket, and pants were gone. God knows what else they did to me, I don't even want to. So, now I have about twenty-one minutes to live, not counting three that I have left from the seven I had today. And it amazes me how even though I haven't had anything to drink or eat for four days now, I still have to go to the bathroom. I'm going to strip off my clothes, light a cigarette, and hope I make it to the nearest dead plant and back before twelve.

Jan. 24, 1999

You'd be amazed how long it actually takes to go to the God damned bathroom. Luckily, my cigarette fell into the freshly watered plant. I'm starting to look like those dead, withered leaves. I haven't seen the sun for two years. I'm really not sure of how this is going to help anyone, but hopefully, the next person who has what I do won't do what I did with my last years. Or, at least, maybe I'll save them from doing what fucking Phillipe did. Do something great. Have sex, go to Las Vegas, get drunk and marry a hooker, find a roulette table and put all your money on the number thirteen and if you win buy a hot air balloon and float around the world in search for the fountain of youth or the most beautiful girl, buy one of those novelty lollipops with the cricket in the middle and eat it in front of all the kids on a grade school playground at recess. Or screw it all and find the most boring thing you can possibly do, so every minute seems like a year. The best advice I have, though, is don't wear a watch anymore. After a while, you won't even need it. You'll know what time it is.

Jan. 25, 1999

I can't remember any of my dreams, and I can only hope that I'm not dreaming right now. I know I've had dreams every night for the past four years, but every night, my dreams become more and more separate from my mind when I'm awake. Not only do I not remember my dreams, but I also don't remember sleeping at all. I'm just becoming myself to my subconscious, so this is the dream, and when I'm not writing, when I'm asleep, that's my reality. I'm just switching over. I don't see anyone else. I don't hear anything besides the low hum of my computer. I want to cut myself to see if anything comes out. I'd be surprised if it did, but I faint at the sight of blood, and well, I'd rather not fall asleep. I'm tired of accepting this inevitable doom. My undeterminable catatonic state is just waiting for the second hand to pass in one more full cycle, and I don't even know if I'm still alive.

Jan. 26,1999

You know what that asshole said? He said, "Dexter, you're a scientific, medical, and psychological mystery, the first living human wonder of the world. Your life will be studied for centuries to come." No, my catatonic body will be studied. My dead, decaying ass will be pondered over for centuries to come. And I'll be the first dead human wonder of the world. I'll be famous and dead, and that's not terribly exciting to me. And what about poor old Phillipe and his tequila-crushed brain? Wasn't he the first living and dead human wonder of the world? Give credit where credit is due. Well, today went fast, a minute faster than yesterday. Good night, soon to be cadaver onlookers

Jan. 27,1999

There's not much left to say, and it's a good thing because I only have six minutes. I can see Phillipe rigging up his death, marveling at his three-minute masterpiece, and thinking of nothing else. That's what happened. His wife and family left him, the same as my fiancé, and outside the world just kept going, but none of that life outside of his room even occurred to him because there wasn't enough time.

Jan281999weareallrushing todeath. Tomorrow i have one minute. And after, if I wake up again,I refuse to waste anymoretime writing. Ddexter nurse deadandwaitingand all out of time

Jan291999

Joseph D. Newcomer is a speculative fiction and social commentary writer and the Founder of DEAD STAR PRESS. His works include *Diminishing Return*, *El Camino Blue*, *Thought & Other Absurdities,* and the upcoming DEAD STAR PRESS release, *Darkest Day*. He started this press to publish and support authors who revel in the weird and, generally, languish in obscurity.

Joseph was born in the blue-collar, Northwest Pennsylvania city of Erie in 1980. Currently, he resides in the Arizona desert, where he continues to write the *Thought & Other Absurdities* blog and podcast while curating his daughter's already impressive comic book collection. Someday, he hopes to be sucked into an episode of The Twilight Zone, though he has a sneaking suspicion that we already were.

Joseph's books are available at DEADSTARPRESS.com, Amazon.com, and JosephDNewcomer.com where you can also find the *Thought and Other Absurdities* blog and podcast. Listen to the *Thought and Other Absurdities* podcast most places you find podcasts.

Connect with Joseph D. Newcomer:
Facebook.com/joe.newcomer.9
Facebook.com/JosephNewcomerAuthor
Instagram and TikTok @josephd.newcomer
Twitter @JoeNewcomer

9.

SEMPITNERALIS

BY

CHARLES PASSMAN

The creature floated and sank at the same time, aimless and everywhere at the same moment, as though sewn into the very fiber of things. It lived in the ocean, part of all oceans, which, of course, were really all one vast, sprawling wunder-work of waters that flowed ceaselessly. The unending flow of the water here made the creature feel soothed and, even in its most frantic moments, calm. If there was such a thing as a narcotic for the creature, it was the feeling of the unyielding currents swirling around it at all times. It could only ever be in any way anesthetized by the water flowing under and over and, sometimes, through deft nook or cranny and even around it. It existed as it always had—without end, without beginning that it could recall. A vast echoing light was its earliest memory, though memory was tricky for the creature to quantify.

Time was harder still, but the light had been a long time ago, and the creature knew that. After the flash-bang of the light, there had been only one thing for what seemed an eternity itself—loneliness.

At the start, it drifted, barely aware of itself, on currents that were not currents like those of the ocean. It was pulled to and fro by the actions of things that now have names—names like physics, gravity, attraction, and chemistry. It existed before these notions, yet, even as it existed, the creature itself supposed by these notions.

Gravity pulled it. Physics determined it might be something at all, to begin with. Although, to the creature's knowledge, which was something less than infinite but greater than finite, it had been something all along. Chemistry had bestowed it with power, which the creature used in its own way—an uproar here, a silent meandering alteration there. But attraction—attraction had brought it here, to its home in the oceans. Adrift in the nothing, it had sensed the oceans.

It slid into the oceans like rain—the creature itself in every drop, plunking down, individualistically yet never less than the whole of itself. That rain had been so long ago, and there had been none but the creature itself to witness it. Sometimes, as so many philosophical beings do, it wondered if there was a grander scheme at play. It often decided there was not. In the water, there were simply currents and tides that it could, of course, influence if it wanted or needed.

But for a long time—much longer than a mere millennium or even several hundred—it simply drifted, letting itself be soothed by the water. Time wasn't so much a line as a bubble. But even at the center of the bubble, always, one could be soothed by the water.

Still, in the peace, there remained the loneliness.

And so, the chemistry came—became useful. An atom or two here, a molecule there, introductions such as a widowed aunt might make between her single niece and a nice suitor.

Here, in this place, there was so much of what would come to be known as carbon, and that was a wonder, along with the water. With carbon and water, and just a bit of patience, one could create the most wondrous things in such a short amount of time.

First, there had been cells, individualistic, feisty, clamoring about, and for the first time, the creature had known something besides loneliness. It knew it was not all that could ever be and never would be again.

Later came all manner of things, all there in the water with it at first—the long giant fish with their silvery bodies, the tiny little amoebas, jellies, and urchins. So much existence to bear witness to!

Then as the oceans circled the sun again and again—sometimes doing this ten or twenty times in the space of a brief nap, it seemed—the creature grew bolder, and the chemistry changed, and the first things wriggled from the water onto the land. The creature had no interest in the land, but the creatures it had begotten might. Watching them *become* turned into a spectacle well worth the watching for many millions of turns around that weak, little sun.

Occasionally, and more frequently earlier on, there were events. Later, these events would be called asteroids and meteors, but the chemistry altered. The air changed. Many of the rocks now burned long before they hit the land or its beloved ocean.

One was especially memorable, albeit sadly, to the degree the creature ever felt sad—it took away too much light for the largest of the land beasts and even those of the ocean—these had been the creature's favorite things so far. But instead of stopping the asteroid, the creature had let it happen, for it had been time, and the creature knew. Past, present, future, these things were all entwined, and it understood when to let something beloved go. By the creature's calculation, the oceans spun around the sun only 172 times after the asteroid struck until the final dinosaur collapsed in a part of what would someday be called Montana. The creature hoped the last dinosaur had not been lonely but knew it had been.

Not so long after, the creature struck upon an idea as inevitable as anything—something else that would not only think and plan and plot, but ruminate as it did, ponder as it did, look at the outward sky with a sense of wonder, as even now the creature did.

Of course, nobody could call the dalliance with 'man' a spectacular success. They were small, lacking the innate, terrible wonder that so many of the species before them had possessed. Nor were they as intelligent as some that would come after, of that the creature was certain. But they possessed the ability to wonder, and that filled the creature with something akin to pride. They made mistakes, certainly. The greed and vice early out of the trees had angered the creature, insofar as it could be angered, and the world had rained again, not with the creature itself but with its tears that it could do so little to guide them. They had ideas and recorded them, passing them from generation to generation, and the creature wanted to shout at them for how much they had gotten wrong, how little they still understood, how little time might remain for any of them to ever know. But the creature understood it could not. It would be like one of humankind trying to speak to a moth.

Still, it watched the humans with interest. They were the first species to not only use and understand deceit but to turn it into a glorious thing, a glamorous thing. Empires were built and crumbled— sometimes the creature drifted off, dozing as it were, and missed such things—Pompeii came to mind. That would have been a sight.

The humans were troubling at times, especially in the most recent few hundred turns or so around the sun—all the chemicals they used and wasted so much of, the ham-fisted 'creation' of nuclear energy—but even more galling than that was the self-righteous pride the species felt for itself in building things they truly believed could destroy everything. Nothing, not even itself, could destroy everything, the creature well knew.

The humans grew in number. At times, overwhelmingly so, but with one wink and a nod at a time to the immortal chemistry found in all this carbon and water, the creature corrected imbalances as they were needed. Wars were invisibly inspired, diseases and plagues would appear seemingly at random and spread. No replicating species could go unchecked—the creature had already tried that with jellyfish many millions of turns around the sun ago, and that had taken ages to clean up.

There were warnings now and then, of course—ice that

shouldn't be melting melted, things that shouldn't be happening happened. Some would be heeded, and some would not, the creature knew. Some would claim religion caused these things and cling to that. Some would claim science and cling to that. Neither was any further right than they were wrong, the creature supposed.

They were a tenacious thing, humans, and scrappy—as violent as the dinosaurs or the sharks, cleverer than the wild cats and climbing vines that found the sun even when born in shadow. They had a while to go yet. They didn't have forever, perhaps, but nothing had forever, not even the sun that this world spun 'round—it only had a few billion of its life cycles left to go. The humans would be gone long before then, of course. What came next? The creature couldn't remember, just offhand. It was content to watch the current programming, so to speak.

Eventually, the sun would dim, and gravity would change, but the creature would be gone before then. It would be adrift, once more, knowing there wasn't a new place to find, for, in some part of it, the next place (and the next after that and the one after that) had already been found.

When exactly it would happen,

where exactly it would go,

all at once,

it both knew and did not know.

Time was such a tricky thing—eternal,

just like the creature

who, surrounded by the waves,

was neither lonely nor alone.

10.

THIS JUST IN

BY

CHARLES PASSMAN

Earlier today, I saw a mustache hurtling down local highways at speeds upwards of the velocity of sound itself. That's right, folks, you heard it here first, a mustache traveling faster than the speed of sound. The mustache was stopped abruptly at the city's limit, where patrol barbers had laid down a multi-straight-edge razor roadblock. After being brought to a flabby halt, a partially nude upper lip, upon being advised of its right to remain silent, subjected both barber and common street on-looker alike to a mumbled jazz fest-esque, unspeakably annoying, pretentious, spoken-word rendition of Jack Kerouac's beatnik classic, *On the Road*. The criminal, formerly known as mustache, is being held without bail or Rogaine at this time.

Charles was born or hatched or landed near New Orleans in the late 1980s - and yes, he was "there for Katrina" - stop asking already! Primarily a performer until now, Charles has worked alongside some of Hollywood's top talent both in front and behind the camera. He currently resides on the U.S. East Coast where he chews cheap cigars (and sometimes even smokes them), and stares dramatically into the middle-distance on rainy days whenever possible. He can, relatedly, be reached at Luvceegars1@yahoo.com, which he tries to remember to check at least weekly. Usually.

Connect with Charles Passman:
Facebook.com/charles.isaiah.12
Instagram @cip59587

11.

DRAIN AND SPIN

BY

DAN SCAMELL

The recycling center always made her nervous. She had heard that the attendants working there were convicts out on work release. They were always civil, sometimes friendly, but she couldn't help but feel like she was being leered at whenever she dropped off her bottles and cans. She was relatively average-looking, though not un-attractive. Blonde shoulder-length hair around a fair face with blue eyes and a chin she thought was too strong. Her thick, runner's legs seemed to be drawing most of today's unwanted attention, though. She was alone now, and this fact made it a great deal more difficult to follow through on her latest impulse. Linda really wanted that washing machine.

While the helpful yet intimidating men were toting the tubs of glass, plastic, and metal from her truck to the appropriate bays, she had seen a pickup, much nicer than her own, pull into the unloading area. It was hauling a trailer full of junk—a glass-top dinner table, file cabinets, an old television, chrome and plastic chairs, a stove, and a washing machine, among other items. As soon as the truck's driver opened his door, Linda was there, intent on getting first dibs on the washing machine if it still worked.

"Excuse me. Sir? Hello," Linda said, as politely as she could.

"Yes, miss? What can I do for you?" replied the driver. He was a broad-shouldered man in his fifties with graying hair under a Mets baseball cap.

"I was just wondering. That washer you have on your trailer

back there, do you know if that works?"

"Well, I couldn't say for certain, but it's just a leftover from an estate sale. We're bringing up some of the stuff that didn't sell yesterday. The boys unhooked it a few days ago before the sale started, so I imagine it was working fine enough."

Linda brightened. She hadn't had a washing machine since before she moved into her new basement apartment eight months ago, and handwashing had quickly lost its novelty. A machine would seriously cut down on the time and effort and probably get her clothes cleaner than washing them in the kitchen sink could. Linda really wanted that washing machine.

"Would you mind if I took it back to my apartment?" Linda started, "I could really use a washer, especially if it's a free washer! My truck is right over there."

"I don't see why not. I can't help you load it, sorry to say. I just drive the pickup these days, but I'm sure the ball-and-chains would be happy to help out a young lady." He chuckled.

"Thank you so much!"

"Glad to help."

Linda reluctantly shuffled back to her truck, where the attendants were stacking the tubs and buckets in which she had brought her recyclables. "Thank you," she said to the closest man wearing coveralls. "I was just wondering if you could help me with one other thing," she said, feeling oddly exposed and trying somehow to make herself seem as unattractive as possible.

"Sure thing, miss," the man replied. "What can I do you for?"

"The man over there," she said, gesturing to the truck with the trailer, "he said that I could take that washing machine. Would you be able to help load it onto my truck?"

"No problem," said the man, tucking his hands back into his

work gloves.

All things considered, things went more smoothly than Linda had imagined. The attendants were respectful and kept their ogling to a minimum or, at least, hid it well. Within five minutes, the washer was sitting in the bed of her truck, waiting to be taken to its new home.

Linda pulled up in front of her apartment building, parked, got out, and moved the lawn chair sitting by the curb that she used to hold her parking space. She backed the pickup as close to her door as she dared, knowing it would just be her unloading the behemoth. In her excitement, she hadn't thought about just how she would get the appliance into her apartment. After standing and staring at it for almost ten minutes, she realized she was just going to have to start moving it and see what happened.

She slid it back and forth across the truck bed, pulling it toward the hitch. When it was hanging about halfway off the tailgate, she started to tip it slowly to the ground, then onto its back. So far, so good. Getting it down the seven steps into her space was going to be more of a challenge. She decided that the easiest way would be to tip the thing on its side and just slide it down the stairs. It wasn't the prettiest method, but it got the job done without scuffing up the metal too badly. From there, it was just a matter of walking it into place. In all, it had turned out to be a far less harrowing experience than she had initially feared. She would have dealt with much more hassle to get it into her home. Linda really wanted that washing machine in her apartment.

The last person who lived in the apartment had taken their washing machine but left the hose hookups hanging from the wall. Linda just hoped they didn't leak. She screwed them to the back of her new washer and turned the water on. They didn't. She ran the machine once with nothing in it, just to see if it worked and would go through all its cycles correctly. After a seemingly successful trial run, she gathered up some stuff to throw into the basin—just towels, socks, and a jacket, nothing that she couldn't stand getting stained or ruined if the machine acted funny at all. When the cycle finished, everything seemed to be in good shape—no rips, no stains.

That evening, Linda went out to pick up groceries for the next few days. In addition to the staples, she also bought a big jug of laundry detergent, bleach, and fabric softener. When she got back to her apartment, she rounded up all the dirty clothes she could find and threw a massive load into the new washer. She set the machine to do a thorough wash, and she retired to her futon in the next room to watch TV and vegetate. The sounds of the washer chugging and spinning helped lull her into a drowsy state. She dozed off.

Darkness. Linda lay asleep as shadows crept across her sheets. In a woozy dream, she could sense them dancing and feel their caresses. Silky tendrils wormed their way up her thighs, tickling the backs of her knees, twirling around her waist. In her mind, Linda was floating in a foamy cove, surrounded impossibly by waterfalls on all sides. She lay face-up on the undulating water as unseen flotsam massaged and stroked her body sensually.

Seaweed slid all around her body, snaking over the curves of her breasts, swirling around her hardening nipples endlessly. Soft, hairlike fibers tickled the sensitive fossae of her arms and moved down to the wrists. Organic threads, seemingly with a hive mind, parted her legs and teased at her labia, gently opening while massaging her clitoris. The touches were rhythmic, insistent, knowing, and gentle—those of an experienced lover who quickly learned what her body needed.

She awakened as her orgasm reached its zenith—her back arching upward lightly, muscles tensing rhythmically. Her body tingled as if the sentient seaweed from her dream was crawling out of and away from her. She lay with her eyes closed, breathing deeply, aware of the dampness in her crotch, beaded on her thighs. She soon lapsed back into sleep, dozing for the remaining hours before her alarm awoke her.

In the morning, while she was hanging last night's load of laundry on makeshift clotheslines strung around her combined living area and bedroom, in the corner of which now sat the washing machine, she could clearly remember the previous night's dream. Recalling the sensations and the feeling of abandon caused her to flush. She had never had such a vivid erotic dream in her life. It was not an unpleasant experience.

Throughout the day at her waitressing job, she had trouble focusing on her work. She brought two of her tables the wrong orders and dropped a glass in the kitchen. She felt worn out but contentedly so. When she got home after her shift was finished, she felt the clothes that she had hung to dry during the day. A fan oscillating on them had done a fine job of drying them, and they were soft, fresh, and clean—much an improvement from her hand-washing methods.

She stripped off her apron and work uniform, then her socks, bra, and underwear to justify having enough to run another load of wash. The washer was a novelty, and she intended to make good use of it. She lay naked on her futon, listening to The Weather Channel on TV and the sounds of the washing machine agitating its contents. Again, she fell from the waking world.

In her subconscious, an unknown figure visited her. It stood at the end of her futon, thin and wispy. She extended her arms and beckoned it in closer. It drifted downward upon her like a fluffed bed-sheet. Its touch was smooth and cool like worn silk, and the parts of it that hung and fluttered like tattered muslin were mystifying to witness. Shreds of its fabric body enveloped her, curling around her ears and tickling her neck. A feathery strip of the being grazed her face and caressed her lips. Another part of its silken body did the same to her lips below. With ease, the entity entered her, undulating inside her, in and out of rhythm, teasing with purpose.

She raised her arms, and the thing danced itself down from her fingertips to her thighs, curling around to her buttocks. She bit down on part of the creature's formless body, grinding it between her teeth as its insistence with her clitoris increased. She came hard, bucking her hips involuntarily while gripping her pillowcase.

Awakening from the dream, she could see a figure in the darkness, more substantial than in her dream, yet still unformed, fluttering in the vague shape of a human. It drifted toward the corner of the room and was gone. Linda was still coming out of sleep and recovering from her powerful orgasm when the thing vanished entirely into the darkness. She vaguely thought she should have been concerned with this but simply couldn't muster the energy to care enough. She plucked a thread from between her teeth.

She called in sick from work the following day. She felt listless and tired. Her manager said that after how Linda acted at work the previous day, she was glad to give her a day off and that she hoped Linda would feel better soon. Following the phone call, she fell back to sleep for a few hours. When she woke up, it was past two in the afternoon, but she couldn't care. She felt satisfied and dreamy.

When she eventually got out of bed, she hung last night's laundry on her clotheslines. With the rest of the day off, she didn't know what to do. She knew that she couldn't stay in bed all day, though the thought crossed her mind. She decided to take a trip to the secondhand thrift shop—she wanted to expand her wardrobe a bit.

She wound up spending thirty-six dollars at the store and came out with four new tops, two jackets, two pairs of black work pants, a pair of striped tights, two skirts, and a sundress. Glassy-eyed, she drove back to her apartment and threw all the new clothes into the washing machine. Six-thirty came around, and it was time to take it in for an early night. The washer was humming and chugging as she lay nude on top of her sheets, running her hands over her skin, feeling a few dry, coarse patches that had appeared—she wasn't concerned with them, though.

She was awakened sometime after dark by the sound of the washer lid closing loudly. She turned her head toward the disturbance and saw someone shuffling out of the corner toward her. He was thin and appeared to be wearing shaggy, loose clothing. Almost without thinking, Linda whispered to him, "Come here." He hovered down upon her, and she could see that he was not wearing anything but seemed to be made from various scraps of fabric and clothing.

She brought the man close and kissed his cashmere lips. Strips of textile undulated about him as if he were underwater. Swatches of denim and wool ran through Linda's hair. Soft handkerchiefs swirled around her breasts. Silk scarves slithered around her calves, lifting and spreading her legs and leaving her prone. Linda gasped, then smiled as she felt the cloth belts latch around her wrists, gently holding her down on the mattress. She knew that what was happening to her was impossible, but she felt so relaxed, so secure with this patchwork man that her mind could accept anything while he was with her.

A twisted braid of threads entered her smoothly, then unraveled inside. A thousand animate fibers spun and curled in time with each other, reaching every nerve deep within her. She resisted the imminent climax already building, wanting to prolong her rising excitement, but soon, the fabric man teased from her a long, racking orgasm that left her nearly unable to move. As the being exited her and pulled away into the darkness, Linda felt a profound sense of loss. A swelling of emptiness. "Please," she sighed, "don't go."

The restaurant had stopped calling after two weeks. Their last message stated that they cared deeply about Linda and were very worried about her, but they couldn't wait on her, and she had been replaced. Linda felt she would miss some of her friends and acquaintances, but she didn't miss the job. She was living off an emergency savings account and the few hundred dollars she had stored away in cash tips.

The weeks had not been kind to Linda. During the times between her trysts with the patchwork man, she became more and more ambivalent to everything around her. Her health had deteriorated as well. She began to develop several rough patches on her skin, some fibrous and with the textures of corduroy or denim. Her blonde hair had lost much of its natural sheen and was falling out in clumps. She was finding herself more and more often picking fibrous hairs from odd spots on her body. Sometimes, they pulled out with no resistance. Other times, they were tough and painful to remove.

She had so little energy during the days that she rarely went out, except to buy new clothes to wash. It had become apparent to her that different kinds of clothing and fabric, as well as different detergents and additives, would affect the tone of her nightly lovemaking sessions. Washing dark, coarse fabrics with powdered detergents resulted in the patchwork man taking her more forcefully and with urgency, while running a load of soft, dainty things with liquid soap and fabric softener would often mean a more relaxed and loving coupling. She didn't prefer one style of lovemaking to another. In the end, it was all just varying degrees of ecstasy.

With bags from Victoria's Secret, Old Navy, and K-mart in her hands, Linda entered her flat, exhausted from the day's shopping and the effort of carrying her new clothing from the truck. She dropped the bags and rested her hands on her knees to catch her breath for a minute, then began slowly pushing the shopping bags across the floor with her foot. She rarely hung the wet clothing up to dry anymore. It was such an undertaking, and she wouldn't be wearing much of it anyway. She had been dressed in the same hooded sweatshirt and pair of yoga pants for several days now.

The pile of wet clothes next to the washing machine smelled stale but not entirely unpleasant. It wasn't worth it to rewash any of it. She had discovered that the clothes, once laundered, seemed to wear out quickly. When she sent the same load through the wash more than once, her lover was more listless and not as attentive. So, she made the trek out to the clothing shops every day or two. So far, she was still able to do that much.

She opened the washer lid and began pulling out the soaked clothing, dropping each article on the pile with a wet splat. After carefully removing all the tags from the new clothing she bought, jeans, t-shirts, skirts, and lingerie she hoped the patchwork man would enjoy, she dropped them carefully into the machine's basin. Organic laundry detergent and lavender-vanilla scented fabric softener were drizzled over the tub's contents. She closed the lid, started the cycle, then leaned onto the cool, metal top of the washer.

Though it was still not dark outside, Linda knew she needed to sleep. She trod to her now bare futon mattress and began to shuck off her clothing. She stood for a moment and stared at herself naked in her dressing mirror. Gazing at herself for the first time in weeks, she now saw more of the changes that had come over her. Her knees were rough, unwashed canvas, badly scuffed, folded into the loose cotton making up the rest of her legs. Her thighs and buttocks were several different kinds of material, poorly sewn together and torn in places. Her public hair was a mat of different colored threads sticking out at opposing angles. She saw that her torso appeared to be a patchwork of pleated wool, dark corduroy, and polyester in a faint paisley pattern. Where her left nipple had been was now a tortoise-shell button, sewn to her cotton stuffed breast.

Somehow she knew that this would have horrified her even as recently as three weeks ago, but now staring at herself like this felt somehow right. She knew she couldn't last very long in this condition, and she couldn't remember how to care. All that mattered now was lying down and drifting into blissful sleep, and then...

The sunlight against her eyelids was what awoke her. It must have been mid-afternoon now. She had slept through the night. The patchwork man had not come. As drowsy as she was, Linda felt a terrible rush of disappointment, then fear for her lover. Had he finally gone away? Was he hurt? Had she offended him somehow? Linda turned over, crawled to the washing machine, and lifted herself to her feet. The dial showed that the cycle had stopped prematurely after the first spin. She opened the lid and saw that the clothing she had dropped in yesterday was knotted and tangled amidst itself. She reached in quickly and began pulling the twists apart where she could see them. A piercing howl shot from the machine basin. It sounded like two out-of-tune violins grinding against each other, made worse by the metallic reverberations of the washing machine tub.

"Oh, God!" Linda shouted. "I'm sorry, I didn't..." Gently, she tried again to untangle the mess of fabrics in the machine, and again came the painful screeching. Panicking, Linda thought that maybe the situation would right itself if she just closed the lid and restarted the wash cycle. She turned the dial and popped it out to begin the next wash and briefly heard the sound of the agitator trying to turn unsuccessfully, then the terrible howling again. She immediately pushed in the dial to stop the machine.

For hours she stood leaning over the open machine trying to gently tug and twist the knotted clothing apart from itself, occasionally stopping when she became too worn out. While she worked, whimpers and screeches came from the twisted patchwork man, but the wet, matted clothing would not give. She sat on the floor and began to cry for herself and her tangled lover. Her tightly woven cheeks absorbed the tears as they rolled briefly down her face.

Though still terribly exhausted, Linda felt a sense of purpose she hadn't since she was first touched by her nighttime visitor. She felt driven to free the poor thing from its soggy, painful prison and began trying to find out how to set things right again.

She researched the washing machine's make and model to figure out how to dismantle it, but she was afraid that tampering with the vessel might dispel the magic it had contained. This would have to be a last resort. She started paging through any phone books she could find to locate appliance repair services, calling some and explaining the situation with her stuck washer. Many of them told her good-naturedly that she didn't need a service call and that she could do as good a job untangling the mess as they could, and it wouldn't cost her anything.

A few of the repairmen actually did come to her house. Some offered to try to untangle the clothes before Linda frantically told them that they couldn't touch anything in the washer. One tried to see if he could dislodge the agitator by pushing and twisting it, and the screeching came as loud as ever. Linda pulled his hands out of the basin.

"Okay, okay!" he said. "Calm down. I was just trying something. Sounds to me like you may have some gears grinding in there, or maybe a belt that's seizing things up."

"Is there anything you can do?" Linda croaked.

"Well, sure. I can take her apart and get a better look at things. Maybe get the agitator out of there, replace what's making that noise—"

"No!" shouted Linda. "I mean, I don't want it taken apart. And I don't want to replace any of the parts. It might... it might not run the same anymore."

The repairman stared at her for a moment, obviously annoyed that he had come out on the call only to deal with some eccentric lady with piles of wet clothes all over her apartment, wearing a full-length hooded raincoat indoors. He sighed.

"Ma'am, I'm sorry, I can't do anything for you right now. I don't know what's in there that's so important, but, um, maybe just start hitting the laundromat." He gazed around at the soggy lumps of clothing on the floor. "They got dryers there too." Then he left.

Most of the service calls over the next two days went similarly—usually less than ten minutes. One man actually billed her. Linda was exasperated and fatigued from worry and lack of proper sleep. Her loins ached. Fingers and massagers did nothing to sate her. She often spent hours staring into the washing machine, sometimes weeping.

Three days after the appliance had stalled, Linda happened upon a phone book that she hadn't seen before in the drawer of an end table. It was over ten years old and covered the area of a city over a hundred miles away, but it was still within driving distance, and she still had a sliver of hope. She went through the appliance repair section and called all the companies. Most told her the same thing—that she could just untangle the clothing herself. Some said that they did not make service calls so far away. None could give her any help.

There was an entry in the phone book that she hadn't seen anywhere else. It was a section simply called General Service with one small ad under it. The ad read, "Zzbyzyx general service. Reasonable rate. House call. Job big and small. 50 percent money-back guarantee. 24-hour service. Call." And then a number. It seemed almost like a joke, but she was desperate and called the number right away, fully expecting it to be out of service. Someone picked up on the second ring.

"Zzbyzyx General Service, how to help you?" barked a gruff woman's voice in a thick accent that was possibly eastern European.

"I, hello, yes," stuttered Linda. She cleared her throat. "Yes, I'm calling to ask about what kinds of services your company offers."

"We offer many services," replied the voice. Then a long silence.

"...Oh, well, I have a washing machine that is stuck and won't turn. The clothes are all tangled up inside, and I, I don't want to pull them apart in the basin. They're very important clothes, and I don't want anything to happen to them."

"Yes." More silence.

"Er, can you do anything to get the clothing unstuck from the washer without damaging it or the machine?" Linda said.

"This is... very important clothes, yes?"

"Yes."

"And very important washer machine, I think?"

"Yes."

"What kind of clothing is stuck?" asked the secretary.

"Oh well, they're just, um, some nice clothes that I consider very important. And I don't want them damaged at all."

"These are nice clothes." It was unclear whether this was a question or a statement.

"Yes, very," Linda said.

"These clothes, they, ah, feels good to wear?"

"...Yes."

"When are you wearing these clothes?"

"I'm sorry?"

"You are wearing these clothes, maybe, at night?"

"I, well, yes." There seemed no point in parsing words.

"Perhaps you are wearing these clothes every night, and the, uh, fabric is feeling very nice on your skin? Make you feel very happy?"

"Yes." Linda gasped.

"I think we can help you. You give me telephone number and address, and I am sending some men to look at your washer machine."

"You really think they can help!" Linda was feeling very hopeful now.

"Your telephone number and address, please."

"Yes." Linda gave them to the woman. "When do you think your men can be here?"

"They will leave here in five minutes. Will take approximately... nine hours."

"Oh— That's very— Thank you."

"Thank you for calling Zzbyzyx General Service. Goodbye."

The call had been placed at 3:30 PM. It was now just past midnight. Linda had tried to get some rest during the evening but only managed fitful naps. She was now once again leaning over, looking into the washing machine. "I think these men can help you this time," she told the wet, snarled load of laundry. "I think we can be together again soon." She ached again between her legs as she gently caressed the soggy clothing.

There were three sharp, loud knocks at the front door. Linda hobbled over as quickly as she could to open it. Standing outside were two men in blue coveralls. Both were tall, though one was very broad and thick, while the other was relatively skinny. The broad one, whose name tag read Yevhen bent his neck down and looked at her.

"You are Linda," he said. His voice was deep, and his English heavily accented like the woman's on the phone was.

"Yes. You're from Zubz, um, Zibbz," Linda tried to remember how to pronounce the name of the business she had called.

The large man smirked briefly. "Yes."

Both men entered her apartment without being invited. Linda was nearly bowled over by the men as they walked directly to the corner where the washer stood.

"It's just... there. Yeah," Linda trailed off, seeing that they were already at the machine.

Yevhen looked into the washer intently for a few moments. "Björn," he said. The other, thinner man nodded and began to look around the apartment as if taking in information.

"So," said Yevhen, turning to Linda, seemingly unperturbed by her odd, fully covering manner of dress. "You have this machine for how long?"

"Almost three weeks."

"You are lucky for this tangle to happen."

"I'm sorry?" Linda said, confused and slightly angered.

"Normally, two to four weeks means death," Yevhen said matter-of-factly.

Björn returned to the washer and began speaking to his partner in a language Linda couldn't discern. He was holding various threads and small scraps of fabric, gesturing around the apartment. Yevhen replied, then nodded in Linda's direction. Björn walked over beside her.

"This likely will be loud," Yevhen said, reaching his hand into the washer basin.

"No! Wait, don't!" shouted Linda, starting to advance on the washing machine before Björn took hold of one of her arms, holding her back. "You can't do that!"

The large man put his arm into the washer tub up to his thick shoulder, then the shrieking began. Behind the wail, there was the sound of tearing fabric, then Yevhen pulled his arm up into view. He was holding up a long, dripping strip of dark fabric, turning it in front of his face and smirking.

Linda wanted to jump on the man, to claw at his face and pull his hair out. He was actually smiling about this, taking pleasure in torturing her lover. It was more than she could bear, but she was held in place by Björn, and in her weakened, exhausted condition, she wouldn't have been able to stop what was happening anyway.

"Stop it now! You're hurting him! Can't you see?" Linda began to cry.

"Ah, so you call it a him?" Yevhen asked. "Do not tell me you have given him a name as well."

Linda was breaking down, sobs racking her entire frail body. "Why? Why are you doing this? What's happening?"

"I am sorry, my dear," began the man. "Perhaps I am being not, eh, gentle enough. You buy this washer three weeks ago. It is working fine. You start to dream about something or someone."

Linda just stared at the man through wet eyes.

"This dream person, he gets maybe bigger or stronger as he every night eh... how do you say?" He looked to his partner for help. Björn said a few words in the men's native language. Yevhen continued. "Yes, at night he fuck you. Then—"

"What the hell do you know about it!" screamed Linda. "Maybe you 'fuck!' That's what someone like you would do! What he and I do—" Linda stalled, looked up to Björn, who was stone-faced, then back at Yevhen, who was now wearing a sad smile. She simply began crying again.

"I know this is not easy, and it makes not very much sense right now. I am trying to tell you. You buy this machine, and inside it is a kind of, eh, demon? Creature? He makes his form of the clothing you wash, then comes alive at night and fu—he sleep with you.

"You feel very good at night, is like painkiller pill. He gives you love, while he takes away what is inside of you. He takes your heart and souls away from you, even your flesh. You are not blind. Have a look at yourself?"

Linda, now sitting on the floor, continued to stare angrily at the man. She had spent too much energy. She could barely even comprehend what was happening at this point.

"Is a kind of trade, he give you very good feelings, but he also takes away everything that you are. You maybe do not believe me now, but you will soon."

Linda couldn't even shout as the man reached back into the washing machine, she just stared as he wrenched out sodden scraps of oddly fleshy fabric. After a while, she couldn't even hear the screams anymore.

It seemed to have taken hours, and, at one point, Linda had fallen asleep. Björn carried her over to her futon, then helped his partner with the task at hand. By the end, both men's arms and chests were covered with filthy, oily liquid, and there were two large buckets full of cloth soaking in lavender and vanilla scented ichor. Linda awoke to see the two men squatting beside her mattress. The thinner was still wearing a mask of indifference, while the larger had a broad smile. He spoke. "So, you are awake now? We have just finished with the hard work." Linda just stared through half-lidded eyes.

Yevhen continued, "I just wanted to apologize for the terrible things you see and hear, but I can tell you, it is all for the best.

"This"—he held up his right arm, clenched in his fist was something the likes of which Linda had not seen before—"is your washer machine man."

She gazed at the thing in Yevhen's hand, her eyes slowly focusing. It appeared to be a sort of skeletal, insectoid creature writhing within the man's tightly clasped fingers. It was about two feet long, and its trunk was maybe a half-inch in diameter with several appendages protruding from it. There was no apparent face or even head on the greasy, black thing. The closest thing Linda could compare it to was a large centipede missing most of its legs.

"Not too handsome now," chuckled Yevhen. "Not too dangerous either, I think. I just wanted to show you what it really looks like, the thing living in your washer machine." The creature he held continued to struggle and writhe and make pathetic whimpering noises. Linda felt sickened, and saddened, and bewildered all at once.

"What, what did you do to him?" she whimpered.

"We did nothing but take off the clothes stuck very tight to its body. They always cry like spoiled children but then never do anything about this. They are rather weak. This is why they must use a kind of, eh, brain magic on their victims."

"It was real! All those feelings were real. I don't want to see him like this. I don't know if I want to live without him." Linda started to weep again.

"Ma'am, this is all not true. You will come to learn what has really happened and how lucky you are that you are calling us." He turned to Björn and barked, "Vidro!" Björn stood and walked over to the washer.

"What happened? What did it want? Why do I... care about him so much?" Linda asked breathlessly.

Yevhen sighed, "They are a parasite. They want to numb you and take your life away. We do not know what happens when they are succeeding. They become the same as us then, I guess—just living life, using their talent to feed on others when they need to. They might live forever or maybe only a month. We cannot know. But when we catch them before this, we can help."

Björn returned to the bedside carrying both buckets. The lavender and vanilla scents were beginning to fade and were being replaced with a rusty, blood-tinged odor. Linda could not see into them from where she lay.

"Now," the larger man began, "you are still very sick, and you are getting better in some days of rest. But you will not become fully better without treatment. We are leaving with you a paper of instructions on how to become well. If you follow these directions, you will grow strong again. Your skin and guts will return to normal, you will not be a torn-up fabric woman anymore. I am leaving this paper on your door, so you can read it when you are strong enough to walk again."

"What about, what about him?" whispered Linda.

"Him? This?" said Yevhen, then guffawed loudly. "Well, we have not any way to kill it that we know yet. Normally, we are putting them in box filled with, eh, cement and sinking it in ocean." He paused, amused by the concern on the woman's face. "Don't worry about it. They are always finding a way back to the mainland eventually. Sleep now. Thank you for your business."

Linda drifted out of consciousness again, this time for the night.

It was early in the morning when she came to, judging from the quality of light outside the high, half-window. Linda was groggy but feeling much better than she had in weeks. Her skin was still a patchwork of old cloth and rags, but her mind was much clearer. She still thought of her lost lover with sorrow but no longer felt a crushing emptiness. She checked The Weather Channel to see the date and learned that she had been asleep two full days. She could not remember having had any dreams. She stood up and padded on woolly bare feet to the front door, where a note was taped. The short walk did not tire her as it would have days ago. She read the note.

Dear Linda,

Thank you again for doing business with Zzbyzyx General Services. Here are directions on how to continue your recovery. When you are fit enough, you must go to one of the automatic laundries listed below. Arrangements are made, and you will be welcome to any of them between 9PM and 5AM, Monday, Wednesday, or Friday night to do your procedure.

When you are going to this laundry, you must bring with you the two buckets of sludge we took from your washer machine and also the jug I left next to your door. It is filled with a kind of fabric softener. With these items at the laundry, find a large industrial washer machine, and an attendant will help you.

Put the contents of the buckets and one cup of the fabric softener into the basin and start the machine. You will then get into the machine while it runs. USE COLD WATER! The attendant will close the lid and open it after the cycle is finished. One cycle should be enough to make you well again. I have not done this, but I am told this is very painful.

Attached to this note is the bill for our services. Please send cash to the address listed when you are able. Thank you. We are happy you did not die!

Signed,

Євген

64

The price on the bill, though not cheap, seemed reasonable to Linda, given that the service that she had received saved her life. The list attached to the note named only four laundromats, and all were at least 250 miles from her home, the farthest being in another country. She didn't imagine she had the energy yet to drive to any but the closest.

Next to her futon sat the two buckets, over half-full each with the matter and liquid from her washing machine. It had now separated. The solids had sunk to the bottoms of the buckets, and a thin layer of yellowish foam had risen to the top. She attempted to lift one and was surprised that she could, if only briefly. Though, when she did this, she felt something give in one of her armpits, and she heard a light ripping noise. She would have to be careful about her delicate skin.

Today was a Monday, but she did not feel up to making a trip, so it would have to be Wednesday. She went back to her mattress and lay down. She still felt that she could sleep a while more, and over the next two days, she drifted in and out of dreamless slumber, occasionally rising to walk around her apartment and reread the note that Yevhen had left her. The "procedure" he had written seemed more frightening the more she thought about it, so she tried not to do so.

By Wednesday, she was feeling quite a bit stronger and was able to move both buckets out the front door and up the stairs. She had sealed the tops with several garbage bags and bungee cords. She didn't know what exactly was inside the containers but knew it was important that very little of it spilled. By noon, she had been able to lift the buckets into the cab of her truck, where she sat briefly to rest her slightly torn-up body. After sitting in her truck for an hour or so, she decided to start the journey to the closest laundromat Yevhen had listed. She traced a few routes in her road atlas and was about to set off before realizing she had almost forgotten the "fabric softener" she needed to take along. She retrieved it and set off on her trip.

The journey was long and slow. Still feeling slightly groggy, Linda had taken a route avoiding highways and as much city traffic as possible. After a bit over six hours, she reached the city where the laundromat was located. It took another hour of searching, but she finally found the correct street. Fortunately, she was not completely out of fuel when she parked outside the building. She was dreading having to pump gas in her condition—not knowing what would happen if any gasoline got onto her new skin.

There was a sign indicating that the laundromat was closed, and all the lights were off inside. Linda was suddenly afraid that perhaps this place had actually gone out of business since the last time Yevhen checked. She exited her truck and walked to the front door. It was 9:40 PM, during the time frame she was supposed to be expected, so she began knocking on the glass door. When no one answered for over a minute, a massive wave of dread surged through Linda. She knocked again, and after another minute, a pair of fingers parted the mini-blinds hanging inside the door. An eye peered at her for a moment, and then the blinds closed again.

"Hello!" Linda shouted. "Hello! I'm Linda. I was told to come here. I was told I would be expected!"

There was a cold silence during which Linda saw herself reflected in the glass of the door. Though still mostly covered by baggy clothing, she could see that her face looked terrible. There were small threads fraying around her eye-sockets and a tear on her cheek through which stuffing was starting to poke. The door opened.

Linda immediately stepped inside. "Thank you! Thank you so much! I'm L—" she was cut off by the woman who had opened the door.

"You didn't forget the sludge did you?" the woman barked. She was small and looked to be either a terribly aged 60-year-old or a sprightly 110. She wore a gray canvas smock and a white head-scarf. Her skin was deep brown, almost black, and ashy. She looked as though she could have stepped out of a black and white television set.

Linda flinched more out of surprise than anything else. "Yes, I mean, no. It's in my truck. Thank you so much fo—"

"Go and get it," the woman said, turning and stepping to a bench inside the laundromat. "I'm an old woman. I can't be helping you with all that mess."

Linda turned and walked back to her truck, shaken but excited. She grabbed one of the buckets, lowered it down to the sidewalk, and then sat on her truck's running board to catch her breath. She was very stiff and could feel the more threadbare parts of her skin being pushed to their limits. It wouldn't be long now, one way or another. She eventually got both buckets and the jug of fabric softener inside the building where the gray woman sat, smoking a long, thin cigarette.

Linda saw a reflective gleam in the back of the room and realized that it was the large washer she would soon be occupying. She waited patiently, standing by the two buckets, swaying a bit on her feet. The other woman lit a second cigarette with the first, then spoke.

"Good job getting them buckets. I seen a few worse off than you, and some a lot less far gone, but you look strong. You gonna be okay." She smiled, which made Linda feel unnerved rather than soothed, and then she inhaled deeply on her cigarette. "Go down the back of the store to the big mama, and take off your clothes. We gonna get you fixed up."

The room was dark, except for the moonlight drizzling in from between the blinds on the windows, the tiny standby lights on the rows of washing machines on the walls, and the cherry of the gray woman's cigarette. Linda shuffled slowly toward the large, stainless steel cylinder against the back wall. It looked like an old-fashioned well, standing nearly four feet tall with a lid on top. There were ominous warning labels plastered all down the right half of it, most warning against precisely what she had come here to do.

A sloshing noise approached, and Linda looked up to see the gray woman trudging to where she stood, a bucket hanging from each hand. Linda would have had difficulty carrying them in her normal condition, but this woman seemed to be having no trouble with them at all. She set them down.

"Now, get your clothes off. Ain't nothing I've never seen before. Don't be shy. You don't want those in there with you when we run the washer."

Linda stripped down and tried not to look at her pathetic, fragile body while the woman unlocked and lifted the large, shiny lid of what she had called the big mama. Linda peered into the machine but could see nothing in the darkness. It smelled of chlorine and metal and seemed entirely ordinary. Looking back up, she saw the gray woman holding out a finger coated in iridescent slime.

"Here you go, sweetie. Have a taste, just like licking your mama's cake batter," the gray woman said, grinning. Linda reluctantly took the woman's finger in her mouth and licked the tar-like slime from it. "I think a little beforehand helps the process along."

Looking at the open jug on the floor, Linda deduced that this was the fabric softener that Yevhen had sent with her. After a few seconds, the taste hit her. It was intensely bitter and burned her tongue. She opened her mouth, but contact with the air just made it sting and burn more. She coughed but kept the fluid in her mouth.

"Now," began the gray woman, "you think you can climb up in there on your own?" Linda nodded. "Good. You get on in there, and I'm gonna start the cycle. It's gonna be cold at first. That's just the water. Then it's gonna start stinging something awful. You ever got stung by a jellyfish?" Linda shook her head no. "Well, good then." She laughed shrilly at this, though Linda found nothing amusing about it. Her head was starting to swim as if she had taken a large, stiff drink.

"The stinging is gonna be the sludge you brought with you. After that, I'm gonna pour in the fabric softener. That's what's gonna do the trick. Just try to remember that in forty-five minutes, this is all gonna be over."

Linda clumsily swung her legs into the washing machine and curled up in the bottom. The washbasin was hard and cold, and there was no agitator in the center. She heard a loud click, and then a frigid waterfall started pouring onto her. The splashing was deafening inside the steel washtub, and the sound reverberated endlessly in on itself. She was on her side, and the water was now covering her arm and part of her lower leg. She could sense her woven flesh beginning to absorb some of the water. Had the deluge not been so bitingly cold, it may have been a pleasant sensation.

The gray woman said something, but there was no way Linda could understand what it was from inside the cacophonous steel chamber. What she could hear was the plopping and splattering of matter falling into the rising water around her. The contents of the buckets she had brought dropped on and around her like wet, oily dough. The smells of lavender and vanilla had entirely worn off of them now, and their scent was stale and sour and offensive. The stinging that the gray woman had mentioned now began. Though her mind felt somewhat clouded, her physical form was still fully responsive.

The pins and needles of a sleeping limb started prodding Linda's body wherever it was submerged. She just barely had her head above the rising water line and, only now, wondered how she would manage to breathe when it came up a bit higher. Above her, she heard another faint call from the old woman assisting her, and she tried to reply, but she seemed to be struck mute by the chaos around her. The stinging worsened. With her head turned up and water starting to flow into her mouth, she vaguely saw the silhouette of the gray woman adding the fabric softener to the wash. Then the washer lid closed.

Too weak to raise her head above the water, Linda slumped beneath it and realized, for the first time in the past hazy weeks, that she actually cared whether she lived or died. It was a comforting yet all-too-bitter realization. Locked inside a thunderous, black basin of rising water and vile solids, freezing sandpaper scraping her skin, Linda closed her eyes and did what she had been avoiding doing. She took a deep breath. Water filled her lungs, and she coughed and gagged, expelling the fluid only to take more in. Her eyes were closed so tightly that they hurt, and she began weakly flailing her arms in panic until she realized that she was not drowning.

The foul water was, indeed, entering her lungs, and there was an intense pressure within her torso, but she was not dying or losing consciousness. Whatever had happened to her, or whatever strange magic or science was now working, was allowing her to live without breathing. Inhaling the heavy liquid still caused spasms and coughing, but she was now aware that she was simply able to stop breathing. Wondering if this meant that she was already dead, she knew there was nothing to do but wait and see.

Very suddenly, the machine stopped filling and became disturbingly silent beneath the water. Linda waited to see what would happen next. She heard a faint buzzing sound, followed by a loud click. After a pause, there was an abrupt and violent whooshing, and Linda could feel pressurized streams of aerated water shooting up from the bottom of the washbasin. The jets were oscillating wildly in place of a traditional agitator.

As the jets worked, Linda's sensory-overloaded mind became

aware that her form was changing. Her body seemed to be deflating or purging itself through her skin. As she became less substantial, the pressurized water started to whip her around amid the now dispersing solids and other liquids in the washing machine. Whatever remained of the bones within her were snapping and splintering feebly. It was what she imagined it would be like to be a large flag in a typhoon, thrashing about at the will of an irresistible force. Fortunately, the searing pain in her flesh had numbed somewhat, either by design or due to her brain being simply unable to comprehend all the stimuli around her.

It felt endless—the droning whir of the washer boring into what Linda could only conceive as her head, the muffled, hissing white noise of the jets rising and falling in intensity, the frigid, stale tasting water on a tongue that seemed very far away now, the darkness. Her body was now nearly incorporeal, just shreds of flesh and fabric and consciousness pureeing in an oversized blender. Pain was an afterthought to Linda now, in the midst of the maelstrom. The dull ache suggested growth, swelling, and connections being made.

The streams of water stopped, and there was eerie silence again before another click and the noise of a smaller motor buzzing. After a moment, there was a long and oppressive sucking and gurgling sound. The poor thing inside the machine slowly sank to the floor of the washtub as all the water drained. As the water level fell, Linda was compelled to cough out some of what she felt inside her, but she could not judge from where to do so. The disorientation was unlike any form of intoxication she had ever known. She felt long, heavy, sodden, tired, and miserable but no longer scared.

As the last of the liquid drained, Linda realized what would be coming next, and she wondered how long she had been in the dark, wet cell and how much longer she would remain there. Once again, there was a click and a whir. The tub began to rotate slowly. The sense of moving without traveling was strong in Linda's mind, and she experienced more a memory of nausea than the actual feeling. The rotation of the spin cycle quickened rapidly and was soon at its full speed—hundreds or thousands or millions of rotations per minute. It seemed to matter little. The pressure was unbelievable. Linda felt herself being thrust against the steel wall of the basin. She felt the water wringing out of her while parts of herself pushed back together and meshed with others. The aching was unbearable, yet it was the ache of a healing wound, and it gave her the slightest glimmer of hope that she may experience life outside of this washing machine after all.

The whine of the electric motor climbed ever higher in pitch until it became inaudible—nothing more than a nagging vibration in the bones. Bones! Linda felt the beginnings of substance forming within her. The shreds and sludge compressed into a solid mass and pressed against the icy metal inside the washer. There were hints of familiarity returning—stiffness in joints, muscles stretching to their limits, a queasy stomach, the faint thump of a heartbeat. There was pain around where her fingernails would be forming. She felt a tugging at the roots of the hair on her head and body. There were cramps where toes began to push through the ends of her feet. She felt her eyelashes tangling.

Realizing she was becoming whole again, Linda felt hot tears where her eyes were returning. She wept for herself now, with the realization of how far removed from humanity she had allowed herself to become. The motor revolving the washbasin clunked off, and Linda could now feel that the tub was spinning with its own residual momentum. It was done.

Her skin no longer felt burnt or frostbitten but, instead, tender as though she lay in a hot bath too long. Chilled to the core and holding her breath, she waited for the spinning to stop. She was eager to emerge but terrified at the same time. Finally, the rotation slowed, and the basin stopped itself. It felt like an hour before the lid clicked and opened.

Linda peered up through bleary eyes and saw the gray woman looking down at her. The woman spoke. "You alive in there?"

After the mayhem inside the steel chamber, Linda could barely hear a word. She attempted to say something but only succeeded in coughing up frigid water and mucus. She thought she could hear the woman chuckling. Darkness fell in the washing machine again, and Linda felt herself being grabbed from under the armpits. The gray woman easily hoisted her up and leaned her over the side of the massive washer. Again, Linda tried to speak but only hacked and coughed.

"Come on then," said the old woman. "Out, out, out."

Linda coughed from deep within her lungs. It was painful but relieving. She brought up a thick glob of ropy black mucus and spat it onto the floor. More followed, but she was soon breathing regularly again. Drooling and glossy-eyed, she looked over at the woman who had helped her. The gray woman grinned and spoke.

"That's right, doll. Get it outta you. That's good. You always gonna have a little bit of that left in you, but that's okay. None of us is perfect!" She laughed again.

"Th-thank you." Linda managed. Her legs were rubbery, and she was barely holding herself upright in the washer. She looked down at herself. Her skin was pink and pruned in places, but it was all there, and it was all flesh. She patted her face, squeezed her forearm, and hugged her breast. She seemed to be all there.

"Now I know you're cold," began the gray woman, "but we gotta let you air dry. Unless you feel like taking a spin in the dryer," she guffawed at her joke. "How do you feel, eh?"

"I'm not sure. Everything is still fuzzy."

"Probably gonna be fuzzy for a few days. You gonna stay upstairs until then. The men already paid me up front, so don't worry about that. You'll even up with them."

It was at that point that Linda finally succumbed to exhaustion. She crumpled over the rim of the washer. The kind woman hoisted Linda onto her shoulder, carried her upstairs to an apartment, and laid her in bed.

It was sunny out when Linda opened her eyes. She was in a mild sunbeam angling through an east window. She felt dry and warm and thankful. The gray woman was sitting in an old, badly re-upholstered armchair in the corner, smiling at her. Linda turned and sat up on the bed, then shakily stood up.

"Now, don't be pushing yourself," the gray woman said as she stood up with the shaky girl. Linda took a few steps toward the woman who opened her arms, afraid the girl would collapse again. The gray woman stepped closer, and the two embraced. Linda let go and returned to the bed.

"I don't know how to thank you," Linda started, "you've been so kind and helpful to me." The woman simply nodded, sitting back in her chair. "How can I ever repay you?"

"Bah," chuckled the gray woman. "Nothing at all. You just pay it forward to the next person you meet needs help, that's all."

Linda looked down at her bare body, its healthy hue had returned. On her left thigh, she noticed something. She ran her hand over it and saw that it was a thick, brown thread. She took it between two fingers.

"Them new fancy, heavy-duty washers sometimes don't do the job perfect, but they're better than the old barrel and washboard," the gray woman said. Then she took the shoulder of the smock she wore and pulled it up over her head. In the morning light, Linda saw that in the woman's youth, she had almost certainly been stunningly beautiful. Now, she sat, bare-chested, skin dry and ashen with a large patch of thick, coarse, blue canvas sewn into her skin from the left shoulder over her breast and down her abdomen.

"Not the color I would'a chose," she chuckled, "but I think you know it's better than the alternative. I got a good pair of shears in the dresser there. We can go ahead and cut that little thread off of you."

Linda gazed at the woman with gratitude and a kind of respect she hadn't felt before. "I think, I think I'll leave it as it is. For now."

The gray woman grinned at her knowingly. "I think that will be fine."

The End

12.

Gorman's Meeting

by

Dan Scamell

The air in the office was too cold. The air-conditioning was running even though it was a cool day. Of course, the office wasn't exactly real in any physical sense, nor was the cold air. They were imaginary manifestations used by the elements of human consciousness as a means to communicate with each other and simplify their jobs. The nebulous morass, which these elements actually occupied, was a difficult concept to grasp, even for them, hence the cold office.

In a chair, which also did not exist, sat Gorman. It was a name given for logistical reasons, and Gorman did not much care for it. Gorman was also given a physical manifestation that was male in appearance. He was indifferent toward it. Gorman was a muse. He worked in the Misery subdivision of the department of Inspiration, which operated under the Creations wing of the Sentience branch of the parent corporation, Humanity.

Gorman had been sitting in the non-existent, existent chair for what felt like a very long time, waiting for his supervisor to enter the room. He had requested a meeting with someone above him to discuss his position in what many called *The Company*. He was displeased with his placement in The Company and was hoping for a promotion or, at least, a transfer. It was not the first meeting he had requested but the first one he had been granted.

At length, the office door opened and Ms. Steele clacked across the hardwood floor of the room on her black heels. The shoes, the floor, and the clacking were not real, but that has already been covered.

"So sorry to keep you waiting, Gorman," she said, wheeling around the desk and sliding into the black leather computer chair there. She was not sorry. She knew that. Gorman knew that. She knew that Gorman knew that. Gorman knew that she knew that he knew that—all part of the facade.

"No trouble at all, ma'am," said Gorman. "I know you're a very busy woman."

"How is your wife?" asked the idea sometimes known as Ms. Steele. She pulled a file folder from a drawer and put it on the polished cherry desktop.

"Fine," replied Gorman. He was unmarried. Ms. Steele knew this. "Thank you."

"So, what topic have we got on the table today?" Ms. Steele tented her fingers, the nails of which were painted a deep and glistening violet to match her hair.

"Well, Ms. Steele," started Gorman.

"Corinne, please."

"Corinne. As I'm sure you're aware, I've been with The Company for a while. I'm very grateful for the work and the opportunities I've been given." He paused. Ms. Steele nodded. "I've been very successful in my department, and I think that I am a great asset to this team. That being said, I feel that perhaps I've done all that I can in my current position. I'm a self-motivated, goal-oriented team player, and I know that I can be of great use to any number of alternative departments." Gorman tried to utilize as much hollow, corporate jargon as he could muster.

Ms. Steele made a show of paging through the thin file in front of her—more subterfuge. She settled on a page and said, "Ah, yes. You're with... the Department of Self-Harm. You've done great things there. I can see your work in razors and cigarette burns are both exemplary. Best numbers in the entire company. A lot of other muses could aspire to be like you."

"Thank you very much, Corinne. I've done my best to make the most of my opportunities here."

"I understand you haven't been terribly happy in your department."

"You do?" Gorman asked. He wondered how much information she had in her file on him.

"Your reviews have noted that your work is well above standard, your bloodshed is on track to break the record before too long, but it's noted that your attitude has been an issue."

"I see," said Gorman. He knew he wasn't happy in his position, but he thought he had kept up the appearance of being an enthusiastic employee. How much did the higher-ups know?

"It's even been noted, and this comes from Rathbone, that your malaise and low morale have been affecting some of your co-workers."

"Rathbone?" Gorman blurted before he could stop himself. Mr. Rathbone was the head of the entire Misery branch. If he heard about Gorman's unenthusiastic performance, it meant that word had gone from the Department of Self-Harm and all the way through Self-Loathing and Woe.

Ms. Steele reviewed the file in front of her, not making eye contact. "Indeed. He's very fond of your work, so he tends to disregard what others have to say about your attitude. You know how some employees can be—sowing seeds of doubt for individual gain. But if you're telling me that you're unhappy here, then…" she trailed off.

"It's not that I'm unhappy here," said Gorman. "It's just that I feel like maybe I've got potential to do bigger things elsewhere. There are other branches of Creations where I feel I'd be a perfect fit. There are many other varieties of inspiration I feel I have the potential to foster."

Ms. Steele smiled wanly. "I see," she said. "Not everything we do here is all that glamorous. I remember when I found that out." She eased back in her chair. "I started in Creations too, in Inspirations, just like you. I used to do a lot of work with humans. Did you know that?"

"I didn't," Gorman lied. It was still cold in the room.

"Art," she said. "That's the one, isn't it? That's where all the muses want to go. We all want to inspire the next great love song. We all want to compel confident brush strokes. We all want to help pen the great poem. But it's not like that."

Gorman listened. He wasn't certain where this was going, but he was afraid of saying something that would dig him into a deeper hole.

"I know, I've been there," continued Ms. Steele. "I've spent a lot of time in several sectors of Art-Creation. I did a stretch in Origami, some time in Mid-Price Athletic-Shoe Design. I was in the Time-Signature department for Junkanoo Music. There was a long patch where I was stuck in Doodles." She was gazing past and above Gorman, who was listening intently.

"I've got a friend who's in Doodles," said Gorman. Ms. Steele ignored him.

"Employees here don't realize exactly how specialized our structure is. Your friend in Doodles, does he enjoy his work?"

"I guess so."

"Does he enjoy the work, or does he enjoy the potential that the work has? That is, does he like inspiring squiggly lines that people draw while they're on the phone, or does he enjoy the fact that he may, one day, compel the pen into the first line of a great work of art?"

"He doesn't really talk much about the actual doodles," Gorman admitted. He had never really thought about whether the work was enjoyable or if it simply had the potential for enjoyment or grandiosity.

"I can't even begin to comprehend the amount of absolute garbage my influence has produced." She shook her head and chuckled. "I must sound so jaded. You know I can't talk this way with most of our workers."

"I guess I never really thought much about it."

"Very few actually do," she said. "The ego doesn't allow for it. I counted the number of shoe designs I inspired one time. It was over seven hundred thousand, just in the time that I worked in the department."

"Wow." Gorman hoped this was the appropriate response.

"Do you know how many of those designs are now remembered?"

"I couldn't venture a guess."

Ms. Steele counted silently on her fingers before speaking. "Three. Do you know how many of those became shoes that any human ever wore?" Gorman was silent. "Zero. Not a single shoe.

"How many ideas, how many thoughts about doing something do you think human beings have a day?" She did not wait for a response. "How many of those do you think they remember? The inspirations that I've conjured, what I had considered would be my best work, nearly all of it was erased from consciousness within days, most times within hours or minutes."

"I—I guess," stammered Gorman, "that's the nature of the job?" He tried to sound sympathetic and knowledgeable without being patronizing. This was his supervisor, after all.

"But it doesn't need to be. Not all thoughts are so easily erased. And that's your gift."

"I'm grateful for the kind words, but I'm not sure I follow."

Ms. Steele eased back in her chair, a thin smile crossing her lips. "How many of the humans you've inspired have forgotten your work?"

Gorman thought. He remembered the subtle nudges he had given to the conscious living, the sour thoughts he had planted, the promises of relief he had made, the ways he had glorified the scent of blood to almost pornographic levels. Many of those thoughts had faded in time, though.

As if reading his thoughts, Ms. Steele said, "Don't think about the task—the active part of your work. Think about what comes after. The lasting effects. After all, isn't that what your friend in Doodles wants? To make something that lasts, something that causes emotion in people? You're in a distinct position, Mr. Gorman.

Gorman considered the long-term effects of his work. He knew that he inspired unease and woe in people to get them to harm themselves, but his conscience typically kept him from dwelling on the effects of his work. Eventually, he spoke. "Scars," he said.

"Indeed." Steele leaned forward in her chair again. "Indeed, Gorman. No other branch, no other department can boast the kind of results you get. There are muses who specialize in grief and self-pity. There are even branches that compel humans to do great harm to each other. But the work that you do, and I'm speaking specifically to you, not just your department, the work that you do is unique.

"A human can heal itself in many ways, both physical and

ethereal. However, this process almost always leaves a mark, a scar. They look down at their arm or their leg every day, and they see the lines of your razors. They see the rings of your burns. Your work. Yours, Gorman."

"My work…" The seas of Gorman's mind were churning.

"Humans see and feel the results of your influence, and it takes them back to a time and place in their lives. They may recall the exact moment that they acted on your compulsions. Smells can do that. Songs can do that too. But they are fleeting, and the human body and mind both acclimate to them in time.

"The impact you make leaves its mark on the body and the soul. One of those marks may fade into nothingness, but both rarely do."

"Ms. Steele," Gorman began, "that's what I struggle with. The, the nature of what I do feels…" Gorman's voice faded into the non-existent frigid air of the room.

"There is no malice in the work of a muse, Gorman. However, you aren't unique in your concerns. This is the Department of Misery, after all, and it takes a certain constitution to make it here. You must take a certain pride in your work."

Gorman thought about human hands grasping sharpened steel, about lighters and matches flaring to life. He remembered the flicking of metal over tender flesh, the way the skin pulled apart so easily when lacerated. Why did it want so much to pull apart from itself?

"I try to do a good job," Gorman said. "There is—" he paused, closing his eyes, which weren't really there.

"Yes? Go on," prodded Ms. Steele. She was leaning forward now with her hands flat on the desk.

"There is a certain…power in it," Gorman finally admitted.

"A fascinating allure. Something mysterious. Something satisfying. But that can't be reason enough."

Ms. Steele was silent, seemingly waiting for more.

Gorman continued, "I know I'm good at my job. And I know why I'm good at it."

"Then maybe"—Steele's voice sounded guarded—"the problem isn't with the work, but with the worker. But that's simply not possible. Our purpose is to give inspiration, spark ideas, compel thought. If we fulfill that purpose, then we have succeeded. If we have succeeded, then we are good. We are whole."

"I'd like to ask you something," said Gorman. He let the question sit and swish in his mouth before speaking it.

"By all means," Ms. Steele said. She sounded like she knew what was coming. She did. Gorman knew she did.

"Do you want to make humans happy?"

"I want to make humans feel," she said. She reclined back into her seat again. "And so do you. That's why you do it. That's why you do it so well."

Gorman thought silently about his work and his motivations. Ms. Steele had raised many points that he had not considered. He had hoped to find some kind of truth in this meeting, but instead, he supposed he had found reality.

"Happiness and goodness can come from many different places, Gorman. It's not our place to discern these facts. I've been waiting for us to have this chat. I had hoped it would not be necessary, but I'm glad to have met with you."

"I appreciate you taking the time to see me," said the muse.

"I can still file for your transfer if you like," said Ms. Steele. "There are promising openings in Marble-Etching, Asian-Male Facial-Hair Styling, Bluegrass-Music Vocal-Harmonies, and Intermediate-Origami, though I can't personally recommend the Origami department."

"I'm not sure." Gorman's voice was distant and thin. "I…"

"It's a big decision, and we hate to lose you. But it is your decision. You can take a little time to think it over. You're owed that, at least, but we'll have to know if we need to think about replacing you." She laughed. "Though, I can't think of anyone filling your shoes. I'll talk with my managers and see what else we've got for you."

For a while, there was no news. Gorman had not made any decision, one way or another. Thinking about transferring to another branch gave him a heavy feeling in his incorporeal stomach. He continued with his work, earning commendations from his peers in the Self-Harm Department without much effort.

He wondered about why he had tested into the Misery Branch and why he did so well with Self-Harm. He had accepted the position without resistance. He thought maybe that he considered it a good stepping stone to something else—painting or singing perhaps. He thought that probably wasn't the true reason, though. He didn't know the true reasons for his current position, and he wasn't keen on thinking too much about them.

Before starting a shift that would be filled with burns and cuts and blisters and bloodshed, Gorman noticed a letter on his desk. Most likely, it was an invitation to a morale-boosting department get-together.

He opened the envelope and read the heading, "NOTICE OF TRANSFER." Well, that was it. The decision had been made for him. There was some comfort in that, but it was also somewhat saddening. There must be some new upstart with great promise set to take Gorman's place—a muse that could sow ill-ease on a greater scale and with more precise skill than himself. He wondered where he was going to end up. He read on.

Mr. Gorman,

We hope this notice finds you well. You have served your department well and done amazing work in your time here. The Self-Harm numbers are higher than we've seen in some time. There are other departments, however, which may benefit from your experience and your work ethic. As such, we are willing to sacrifice the terrific work you do with your current department in order to take a chance with you.

We have contacted other branches and departments to get their input. Incidentally, your name and work precede you. After careful consideration, we are pleased to announce our decision, effective immediately. It gives us great joy to inform you of the next step in your great journey. We hope you will carry on from your previous work, your succinct devotion to this new assignment. Mr. Gorman, welcome to The Department of Suicides!

The End

13.

An Impolite Evolution

by

Dan Scamell

I was too polite to say no. At first, I thought they were Jehovah's Witnesses or Mormons or whoever else goes door to door to peddle religion. I heard Prince was a Jehovah's Witness. I heard he showed up at some people's door one day to carry the message. That would have been awesome, to have Prince knock on your door out of the blue. Supposedly, he was only like, four and a half feet tall. I'm getting off-topic.

The people who came to the door asked if they could have a few minutes of my time, and I let them in. They seemed nice—a man and a woman in powder-blue slacks and black dress shirts, each carrying an old-fashioned kind of briefcase. Classy leather deals, almost like you'd carry a bowling ball in.

We sat in my living room and chatted for a while about dumb stuff like the weather before the pair got to business. The man, I can't remember his name, asked if I thought that our society was taking responsibility for its actions. Here we go, I thought, anticipating a conversation about Jesus or the rapture or maybe some environmentalist scheme. I'm polite, though, so I let them talk.

The woman, her name was Jessica, I remember that. Jessica asked me what I thought a society's responsibility was. I tried to answer right. I said that I thought that the members of a society ought to be interconnected and helpful to one another, regardless of their differences. I used to actually think that, then later, I mostly just thought people should leave each other alone. Let everyone do what they want, but take care of the troublemakers, of course. Can't have a bunch of assholes running around.

Jessica told me that a good society thinks of things other than itself. So it is some tree-hugger thing. She said that we, as modern humans, owe our very existence to the challenges provided by other creatures and natural factors, that man owes a thank you to all the bears and poisoned frogs and venomous snakes and storms and fires that made us the creatures that we are. I agreed, to be polite. I didn't really follow, though.

It wasn't fair, they said, that humans had taken away so many of the hardships that made them what they are today. And in doing this, we were stopping other beings from coming up and having a chance at having what we've had. The man said that humankind was doing a good job at creating hardships for most other living things on the planet, but we were doing it far too quickly. We weren't really giving a fair chance to animals and plants that, given enough time, could be the next apex beings of the planet.

I let them go on and on about their agenda. I didn't really understand most of it, but I said it sounded very interesting, and I agreed with a lot of what they said. After they had finished their sales pitch, Jessica asked if I would be willing to accept a "gift-of-service" from them. I said, of course. I would do whatever I could, given my busy schedule. At first, I thought she was very pretty. When I remember her now, I guess she looked good, but kind of like a cousin or something, maybe.

They said that they would leave one of their leather briefcases with me. The man told me that even if I didn't follow through with my service, that I could keep the case. I liked that. Jessica went out to her car down the street and brought back a new briefcase for me. It was in a sealed plastic bag. Brand new! I loved it immediately. They left me with a few pamphlets and set off down to the next houses on the block. I watched out the window for a while. I didn't see anyone else open their doors for the duo. No one else in this neighborhood tries to be polite.

So the next day, after walking around the house with my briefcase, pretending I had somewhere important to be, I read one of the pamphlets. It had a bold heading that read THE HANDICAP! It was all about trying to even the playing field between all living creatures like plants and animals and insects and humans and everything. The pamphlet was narrated in speech bubbles by a cartoon brain-looking...thing. It gave statistics that I don't really remember. Stuff about how long it takes an organism to evolve naturally and how that would not be possible now that humankind was so far ahead of everything in so many areas. It sort of made sense. I guess. I don't really know. I liked the cartoon brain. One drawing had an arrow pointing to him from the words "Mr. Goozle."

Oh, and it said THE HANDICAP! was an entirely natural and beneficial event that would be in the best interests of all living creatures. The brain, Mr. Goozle, said that comets hitting the Earth were good handicaps, that ice ages were very good too. The biblical flood was a very good one, except that God had played too much favoritism in that case. When Mr. Goozle said this, it was holding an umbrella in its little, nubby spinal cord. I laughed at this. I laughed so hard that I fell over, actually.

According to this literature, the answer wasn't to wipe out humanity or any other creature, but instead, it was to incapacitate them and make them care less about stuff, stuff like learning and reading a lot. It said, especially, that sex was something that living things shouldn't be too concerned with. It said that being celibate was wonderful, that being gay was good too and that being bisexual was acceptable but not ideal. I wasn't sure how I felt about that, but it seemed to make sense. Babies cause lots of problems, and making them is a lot of work.

Another pamphlet was all about what it would be like with everything on a level playing field with humankind. I read one particular section over and over. It was about how great it would be to see a movie written by, produced by, directed by, and entirely created by ants. It would be a totally new experience for men and women. I never thought about it before, but I found myself wanting to see this ant-movie. I cried a little that I had never had the chance to see one, but then I stopped crying and took a nap.

Oh, right. I opened the leather case they left me. There was a little brain in there. It looked like a brain anyway, like Mr. Goozle. I liked looking at it. Whenever I looked at it, I wanted to touch it and pet it, and my head felt warm and nice, and also warm. I petted it a lot for a few days after they left it with me. It felt like a rubber glove filled with wet sand. There was a leaflet about how to care for the brain, which was called a Goozle. Mostly, it said to just be nice to it and do whatever you feel like when you're around it and to bring it around to other people's houses. Better yet, it said, have other people come to your house to see it. Also, put it on your head a lot, especially at night or whenever you feel like sleeping.

I've had Mr. Goozle (I named it after the one in the pamphlet) for a while now, and I feel nice. The other day after wearing it on my head like a hat for a few hours, I set the neighbor's house on fire. It seemed like something good to do. I knew that Mr. Goozle wanted me to do it. Also, I haven't mowed my lawn in a while. Fire was a good handicap, according to the pamphlets. The two people who left the Goozle with me would probably have wanted me to set the fire, and I don't like to be impolite. It wasn't a big fire, and the neighbors thought it was from their dryer vent.

I got a girl from the grocery store to come to my house. I had Mr. Goozle in my shopping bag, and I think being close to it made her feel the nice, like I did. At my house, she seemed to think that I wanted to have sex with her. I said no, I didn't really like that kind of thing, but that she could masturbate if she wanted to. I cut my thumb off because it felt like something Mr. Goozle would want me to do. I got the grocery store girl to wear him as a hat for a few minutes. Then I cut off her thumb too. She didn't like it at first. She didn't have as much of the nice Goozle-feeling as I did, after all. But she still let me do it.

Oh yeah, I was at the grocery store to buy vinegar. If you pour vinegar on plants, it kills them for a while. After her thumb stopped bleeding, the grocery store girl and I went into the woods and poured a few gallons of vinegar around, so the plants up there didn't get too far ahead. The one part of the pamphlet said that there are so many plants that it's okay to hurt them sometimes to keep things even. It said that they were probably going to take over after humans if they could stop being so lazy.

I had my neighbors over for dinner. They were living in a hotel until the fire damage in their house was fixed. I made mashed potatoes and chicken. I made sure not to cook the chicken too long. Sickness is a good handicap for people, the pamphlets said. I laughed a lot that night. It was fun. Terri, Mark, and their baby were here for the meal. I don't know the baby's name. I don't even remember if it's a male or female baby. It's really ugly.

I have a ceiling fan above my dinner table. I taped my little friend to the top of the fan and turned it on low. Mr. Goozle spun around and around above our heads, and Terri and Mark started to feel the nice from it. They asked me what had happened to my thumb, and I laughed. I laughed and told them it was okay because I never wanted to be a movie critic! They didn't laugh at first, even though I told a joke. Remember those guys who reviewed movies? They had thumbs. Maybe they didn't get the joke. It would have been polite for them to laugh, though.

We talked about the fire for a little bit until the Goozle feeling started to sink in for them. I could tell when they started feeling the warm and the nice. They got friendlier then and ate the under-cooked chicken without complaining. I showed them the literature that the people had left at my house, but they didn't quite understand. I wished that Jessica and the man were here to help explain. After a while, I took Mr. Goozle down from the ceiling fan. We all laughed about that, and I washed the dust off of him.

Terri and Mark wished that they had a Mr. Goozle now too. I knew it was impolite, but I didn't want to give them mine. The in-structions that came with it said that you could cut the Goozle in half, and it would grow into two Goozles after a while. I told them we could do that. I was scared to hurt my friend, but we went ahead and cut him in two.

One piece was bigger than the other, and I gave them that half. I wanted the bigger part, but I guess it was nice to let them have it. There were three of them, after all, for now. I told them that they should get rid of their baby, that babies cause problems, and when they grow up a little, it makes you want to make more babies. They weren't too keen on that. I think they'll come around after a while.

After they left, I looked at my little half-a-Goozle, and I was sort of sad. I wanted to have the whole thing, but this one would grow up big and strong again one day. And half a Goozle was enough for the grocery store girl and me. She lives in the basement now. Sometimes we sleep on the floor down there. I wanted to sleep in the bed with her once. Mr. Goozle didn't think that was a good idea, so I went up to the attic and rolled around in the fiberglass insu-lation.

The grass outside is really tall now. The grocery store girl and I started a big fire in the woods. Not really to hurt the trees, but to make a lot of smoke that would get into the air, so we didn't breathe so good. I guess it wasn't a really big fire, but it was okay. Some smoke went into town. I leave a lot of garbage outside my house so that maybe bears and raccoons will eat it. The fire department put out the fire we made. I hope they go away. Maybe we can set the firehouse on fire. That would be funny!

Jessica and Tony came back to the house today. His name is Tony, I remember now. He's better looking than Jessica too. They said that I had been doing a really good job with the handicap stuff. They asked if they could take the Goozle back now. I felt mad that they were being taker-backers, but I didn't want to be impolite, so I let them have it.

They explained that enough time had passed that I would always have the nice, warm brain-feeling now. It was true. I didn't pet Mr. Goozle or wear him much anymore, and I still felt the nice. They said that if I gave him back, they could give it to other people and make them feel good, that it was all part of the process. They said I could still keep the leather case, though. I was glad about that. I had already filled it with parts of a dead deer I found a couple weeks ago.

I told them about my neighbors and their half-a-Goozle. They were happy about that and said that they hoped that Terri and Mark had cut that one and given some to someone else. I told them gravely that they still had their baby. Tony and Jessica seemed to think that was okay. They thought that eventually, Terri and Mark would realize how much trouble their baby was and get rid of it. They said that they were going to see Terri and Mark after they talked to me.

Tony thanked me for my service and said that if it wasn't for me, they wouldn't have made nearly the amount of progress in this neighborhood that they had. He shook my hand, and I started to blush. Jessica said that I had done great work for the handicap and that I could keep it up if I felt like it. She also said that it was good if I wanted to watch television and sleep a lot. Those were part of the duties as well.

As they were leaving, I told them about Grocery Store Girl. She couldn't come up from the basement, though. She had a ton of maggots in the gash in her leg, and if she moved too much, it would disturb them. I let them rest down there and said her goodbyes for her. I thought it was the polite thing to do.

The End

14.

WINSTON AND RAYMOND

BY

DAN SCAMELL

Winston was on the couch, listening to Raymond talk about what had happened to him at work. Winston was a good listener. The telephone receivers that were his ears came from phones that had barely been used. Raymond, whose ears were made of skin, cartilage, and bone, wasn't necessarily a good talker. In fact, he barely spoke at all if he didn't need to. But he liked talking to Winston. Winston was his friend.

"So, I had to deal with this old lady at the supermarket today," Raymond said. "She came down the aisle I was stocking to ask me about tuna. She was asking about why the tuna cans were so expensive even though they were supposed to be on sale this week. I told her that the kind that was on sale was the store brand, not the Starkist. She's like, 'Oh, well, my cats won't eat the store brand. They only like the good kind. It's supposed to be on sale!'

"I tried again to tell her that she made a mistake and that it was the cheap tuna that was on sale, but that we were out of it. Oh, and the whole time she was staring at my hat." Raymond referred to the black knitted cap he had taken to wearing low over his brow after he had drilled the first hole in his head.

"That seems odd," Winston said in a thin voice from the electronic speaker serving as his mouth. "Are you sure she was staring at it?"

"Yeah, as if she'd never seen anyone wear a hat before." In

reality, the old woman hadn't been staring. She had glanced at it a few times, thinking it odd that the supermarket would be okay with their employees wearing plain, black knit caps, which she thought gave people a somewhat menacing look. "So, she keeps telling me that she can't afford the good kind and that the flyer said that it was on sale. Eventually, just to shut her up, I told her I would mark down the cans to the sale price anyway."

"That was nice of you," said Winston. "Are you allowed to do that? I'd be afraid of getting in trouble."

"I got in trouble last time I did it, and I probably will this time too."

After a pause, Winston responded, "I guess I understand that. I would be worried that the customer would get mad at me if I didn't give them what they wanted. I would want them to like me."

"That doesn't have anything to do with it," Raymond said.

"Oh."

"I just hate arguing with these morons, and giving them what they want is the best way to get rid of them. They know, though," said Raymond.

"They do?" Winston asked. He wasn't sure what Raymond was talking about.

"Yeah, they hone in on me all the time because they can sense that I'm a pushover. It's written all over my face that they can take advantage of me, and they do."

"Does it bother you that you're a pushover? You could stop being that way."

"It doesn't bother me, it's just"—he searched for the right word—"annoying. And I can't just stop being that way. It's like, I don't know. It's part of how I am. I try not to be that way sometimes."

"Is it scary?"

"No! It's just hard to be different than the way you are. It's easy to just go along with people."

"It sounds like it would be scary not to be a pushover."

"So, I start marking down these cans for this stupid lady, and she's like, 'Not those cans! They're all dusty. How long have those been there? Don't you rotate stock? Can I have ones that aren't dusty?' and on and on. She ends up picking out twenty cans."

"Is that a lot?"

"It's a lot to mark down without a manager. I'll definitely get in trouble."

To Winston, Raymond sounded almost as if he welcomed the idea.

***

On Saturday afternoon, Raymond went to the hardware store. He bought an assortment of supplies for Winston, for whom he had promised to build a proper body. He kept sweating the entire time he was at the store, even though it wasn't warm there. An employee had asked him what he was building and if he could be of any help. Raymond didn't want to tell the man the nature of what he was building and couldn't think of a good lie to tell the smiling man on the spot.

Raymond knew that the man, whose name was Reggie, was suspicious of him from the beginning. He knew that he was building something secret and embarrassing. He was also staring at Raymond's hat. After receiving some desperately unwanted help, Raymond thanked Reggie too loudly and quickly and turned to keep looking for what he needed to buy. He picked up some lengths of threaded rod, pipe, springs, nuts, bolts, hinges, wire, D-cell batteries, duct tape, and a small level, among other things.

When Raymond paid at the counter, his debit card wouldn't read correctly. He swiped and swiped, but the card wouldn't work. His brow creased deeply in frustration. He hated the card for not working. He hated himself for owning a debit card that didn't work correctly one hundred percent of the time. He hated the cashier for standing there while he continuously embarrassed himself with his malfunctioning plastic rectangle. Sweat dripped off his nose onto the counter, and he knew that the girl working the register was disgusted by it. She would probably tell her friends and coworkers about the gross, weird customer she had earlier. Raymond would have to use a different hardware store for a while.

At length, the card worked. When he got home and pulled into his driveway, Raymond saw that his neighbors, Pam and Andy, were sitting on their porch. They would talk to him. They would ask what he bought and what it was for. Eventually, he got out of his car. He had probably stayed in it too long. They were probably thinking about how weird it was that he was sitting in his car. He attempted to grab one of his bags and rush into the house without interacting with the neighbors, but it was unavoidable.

"Hey Ray, whaddaya say?" called Andy.

"Good morning," replied Raymond. It was 4PM. Andy and Pam seemed unfazed by this gaffe. They would probably be talking about him later—after he was inside.

"You busy? Want to sit and have a beer with us?" Andy chuckled, "Well, I'm having a beer, this one"—he motioned to his wife—"is having some kind of pink, fruity nonsense."

Pam laughed. "Oh yeah, he talks tough, but every time I buy a six-pack of these, I'm lucky if I get two before he finishes them all himself!"

Raymond barely heard what they said, already trying to formulate a polite refusal. "I'm don't think so," he said. *Stupid! I'm don't think so?* he contemplated his linguistic failure and hurried inside.

"Stop by if you change your mind," said Pam.

Inside, Raymond set his bag on the living room floor. He had two more bags in the car, but he didn't want to go out and have to interact or awkwardly ignore his neighbors after what he felt was a major embarrassment. He would wait until they went inside to get the rest. He'd just let them talk about him for a while.

After dark, Raymond got the remainder of his supplies and started constructing a body for Winston. At the moment, Winston was simply a stainless steel pail with a bolt through its bottom. The pail had holes drilled through it for eyes, ears, and a mouth. His eyes were two bulbs from a string of Christmas lights, and his mouth and ears were old cell phone parts. Each of these components had wires dangling from them into the bottom of the pail. Sloshing in the pail was a small amount of water mixed with tiny bits of Raymond's own brain tissue and a couple of double-A batteries. Winston was named after the word embossed on his forehead—the name of a kitchen equipment manufacturer.

Winston watched as Raymond built him a spindly, steel body with springs and hinges for joints, clamps for hands, blocks of wood for feet, and copious amounts of duct tape. "You don't have to do this," he said.

"You need a body so you can walk around and... I don't know. You should have a nice body."

"I'm really okay the way I am. I'm used to it. It's the way I am. I'm a little afraid of what it will be like with a body. What if I'm not the same anymore?"

"Why wouldn't you be the same? You'll still be you, but just better."

"I don't know if I want to be better."

"We'll just try it out and see how it is," Raymond said as he put the final touches on the new body. The last thing he did was duct tape the level to the steel rod shoulders so that Winston would be able to keep his balance while walking. He took Winston from the couch and spun his bolt-neck into the new body's shoulders. "There," Raymond spoke proudly. "How do you feel?"

"I don't know," replied Winston after a long pause. "It's different and kind of weird," he said as he sat awkwardly on the couch.

"I know, but you'll get used to it. I'm gonna do some brain surgery again now, so I need you to be patient for a while."

"Okay."

Raymond went into his bathroom, where he now kept his power drill. He knew that he would have to drill a new hole into his head to get at a different part of his brain. Obviously, the talking and reasoning part of his brain wasn't in the same place where the balance and walking part would be. His best guess was that this stuff would be on the left—the side opposite where his current hole was. He hoped that the procedure would go a little more smoothly now that he had some experience.

After cleaning the masonry-grade drill bit in alcohol, Raymond picked a spot on the left side of his head above his ear. He put the drill tip to his scalp and started the process. He had set the drill to go as slowly as possible so as not to bore too far or fast. After a few seconds, the familiar pain came—the pain of tearing away skin with hardened metal. The blood began to flow, but he was ready for it this time and wouldn't panic at the volume of hot fluid running from his head.

Within a couple of minutes, he felt the familiar grinding as the drill started to scrape away at his skull. Working closer to his ear made the sound far worse this time, and the vibrations threw off his equilibrium. He had to stop a few times to steady himself, as well as to clean the drill bit of its muddy coating of blood and bone dust.

As he had expected, it was a slow process, but it seemed to be going much more easily than before. He had vomited three times before completing his task the first time, but this time, it only happened once with some intermittent dry heaves. As the flared tip of the bit went deeper, it began to chip away small chunks of bone. He fought to keep the drill steady as it caught on jagged edges of the tapered hole. Raymond knew that he had to just keep at his task until it was done and trust that he wouldn't start a crack or slip the bit through the growing hole in his skull.

Finally, the chipping stopped, and the drill tip spun smoothly in its small, round hole. That was far enough. He gave himself a few minutes to sit and recover before walking back out to see Winston.

"Are you okay?" asked the metal man.

"I'm fine. How are you?"

"Fine."

"I'm gonna open your pail for a minute, okay?"

"I know."

Raymond sat next to Winston on the couch and pulled out what appeared to be a tiny melon-baller on a narrow rod. He gingerly stuck the round end of the device into the freshly made portal to his brain. He spun the rod and retracted it. There was now an orb of pasty matter in the melon-baller, no larger than a baby aspirin tablet.

He removed the top of Winston's pail and tapped the small round blob into the bottom. He repeated this process twice more, and as he did so, he made sure that he thought hard about walking, balancing, and climbing stairs. After he finished, he retrieved the batteries he had bought and plunked two of them into Winston's head. A full body would take much more juice to power than just a head. He then went to the kitchen and got a few ounces of water in a cup to add to the pail. Everyone knows that water is the key factor to life.

When everything was all set, Raymond closed the lid of the pail and sat next to Winston. "How are you feeling now?" he asked.

"Okay."

"Do you want to try to stand up?"

"I don't know."

"Give it a shot."

"Okay."

Winston uneasily rose to his wooden block feet, grasping on-to anything in reach for balance with his clamps. After a few minutes, he was standing erect on his feet, testing his balance, and seeing how far he could bend and lean. He turned to face his friend. "Can I sit down again?"

"Try to walk around a little."

"Okay."

Winston slowly wobbled around in a small circle until he got the hang of the motions. "Raymond," he said.

"Yes?"

"I think this might be okay."

***

Winston and Raymond sat on the sofa having what Raymond liked to call "class." This involved running a long, spiral telephone receiver cord from one of the holes in his head into Winston's pail. Raymond had figured that this would be a safer and easier way to transfer his knowledge than continuing to drill holes in his head and scoop out bits of brain. This was also a good time to chat.

In the past couple of days, Raymond had painted his friend's metal face with several coats of specialty enamel which was meant to work as a dry-erase board when it cured. He had also tied a dry-erase marker to a string and tethered it to Winston's shoulder so that he could draw on his face to reflect his mood.

"Why are you so afraid of the neighbors?" Winston asked. He had used the felt end of his marker to remove the neutral face from his pail and had drawn a weak frown and upturned eyebrows.

"What?"

"You're scared of Pam and Andy and a lot of the other people who live around here."

"I'm not scared of them. Why would I be?"

"That's what it feels like when we have class. I think I can feel a lot of the stuff that you do, and when we think about seeing or talking to people, I get scared."

"Well, I'm not afraid of Andy and Pam or any of the other people around here." Raymond paused. "I mean, I think they're annoying. I just get frustrated when they try to talk to me."

"Why?"

"Because they're all assholes. They think they're better than everyone else, and it pisses me off."

"So, you're mad because they are wrong?" Winston thought a moment. "Are some people better than others?"

"No, it's not really like that, exactly. I don't know how to explain it."

"Are you better than Andy and Pam?" Winston asked, opening and closing his spring-clamp hands. He did this when he was nervous or confused.

"In some ways, I think so. I respect other people's privacy more than they do. I don't feel the need to speak to every single person I see and talk about myself all the time."

"Talking to people is bad? It seems kind of nice."

"It's a hassle. I never know what to talk about, and I don't have anything interesting to say. I just try to save everyone the trouble of having a dumb conversation by staying quiet most of the time. I can't relate to people like that."

"Is it bad to talk about yourself? You talk about yourself a lot to me."

"I can relate to you—we're friends. You like asking questions and learning. Nobody else cares about that stuff. People just think they know the answers to everything already and that everyone else is stupid." Raymond rubbed the bridge of his nose between his thumb and forefinger.

"You feel kind of sad. Are you sad now? I'm sorry if you feel sad."

"I'm not sad—I'm just tired."

***

The line at the pharmacy counter was several people deep, and Raymond was right in the middle of it. He hadn't been able to refill his prescriptions on the internet. The system on the website didn't work right. Nothing ever worked right.

There was a young woman on her phone in front of Raymond. She was seemingly unaware or uncaring that everyone could hear her conversation.

"My professor is just an asshole," she said into the small electronic device in her hand. "He failed me on my last paper and won't even tell me what I need to do to fix it... I know... Like, aren't you supposed to be teaching me? I'm paying for this dumb class, and when I do what he wants, he fails me."

Raymond wished he could tune out the noise and considered leaving the pharmacy and coming back later, but he had already made it this far and didn't think he'd have the energy to leave the house again for a while if he went home. He was sweating again. Everyone could probably smell him.

"I cited my points and explained everything exactly how I was supposed to. Just because he's an idiot who doesn't agree doesn't mean he can fail me. Oh, and apparently Wikipedia isn't a valid source." She laughed loudly.

A heat was flooding Raymond's face. He was getting unreasonably angry, and he knew it.

"Yeah... I'll probably file a complaint. The department head likes me, so it should be fine."

Later, at home, Winston listened to Raymond recount the event. Winston had a lot of questions but wanted to be careful what he asked, so he didn't make his friend angry or sad or tired again.

"She sounds kind of rude. Did you walk away and come back later?"

"No!" barked Raymond. "I shouldn't have to do that. She should know that no one else wants to hear her idiotic conversation about how stupid she is and how she's failing."

"Did you go to college?"

"*I* didn't have the money. Lots of people don't get the opportunity, and if we did, we wouldn't bitch about inane bullshit." There was scorn in Raymond's voice now. Winston was getting nervous that he was making things worse. He stood up and paced around the room, flexing his clamps. The telephone cord connecting him to his friend bounced and wobbled. "And she was trying to work out a way to get her grade changed."

"That would be good for her"—Winston paused—"right?" He erased the subtle smile he had been wearing and drew a bigger one. He thought it would be more appropriate.

"People need to learn that you don't just get to have everything you want all the time. You need to be able to take what's given—take the hand you're dealt."

"Is that what you would do?"

"Sure! I'd realize that I had made a mistake, and maybe I wasn't even smart enough for college."

"You would quit?"

"I know when to quit. I live within my means. I don't pretend I'm special or better than other people. That's why I keep to myself. I don't *need* a ton of fake friends. I don't *need* a fancy job. Everyone has such skewed priorities. They don't have any concept of what really matters."

"What really matters?" Winston asked softly. There was a long pause, and Raymond furrowed his brow. Eventually, he stood and removed the telephone cord from his head. He picked up his cell phone and made a call, then turned back and spoke to Winston.

"Pizza."

Winston wanted to change his smile to a frown but didn't want to upset Raymond.

***

Clump. Squeak. Clump. Clump. Squeak. Clump. One of Winston's foot hinges squeaked a bit when he walked. It didn't bother him too much. Lately, he has spent a lot of time walking and thinking. He looked out the windows from time to time, admiring the outside world but never wanting to enter it. There was a lot of stuff out there—a lot of people. It was scary.

He was feeling somewhat lonely but also enjoying being alone with his thoughts. He wanted Raymond to come home soon, though he knew that when that happened, Raymond would probably complain about a lot of things that the metal man didn't quite understand.

Winston knew that his friend was unhappy and wanted to help him, but he couldn't figure out how. Most of the time, when he tried to make a suggestion, Raymond would simply shoot it down and explain why the world didn't work the way that Winston thought it might. It made Winston feel dumb and wrong and bad. Raymond seemed to be okay with just being mad and scared and complaining about stuff. Being unhappy seemed to make him, in some way, happy.

Clump. Squeak. Clump. Clump. Squeak. Clump.

This was the conundrum that Winston pondered most times when he was alone. Winston wanted Raymond to be happy, but things that he felt made Raymond happy made Winston unhappy. Winston was starting to wonder if he was supposed to be happy. Maybe Winston was just supposed to be uncomfortable and disappointed. Maybe Raymond *was* correct about how the world worked. It didn't seem right, but Winston trusted his friend, who surely knew more than he did.

When Raymond talked about the things that annoyed him, they often involved other people feeling good. Conversely, a lot of the time, the stories of others feeling good made Winston kind of happy. He liked hearing about people having fun or doing things without fear or anger, but he stopped drawing smiles on his face when he heard these things. He knew that wasn't what Raymond wanted to see. Raymond always spoke as if all the people he interacted with were wrong about things. Winston believed him for a long time—it seemed like Raymond was right at first. But now, he couldn't help wondering if maybe other people knew something that Raymond didn't. He wondered if Raymond would be happier if he would try to learn from them instead of complaining about them all the time. Winston liked learning. He didn't know if Raymond did.

Clump. Squeak. Clump. Clump. Squeak. Clump.

The water and brain matter in Winston's pail-head sloshed around as he walked. He sometimes worried that he might fall over and spill the contents of his head. He felt like the lid of his pail held pretty tightly most of the time. Raymond was always careful to secure it after he had had it open for class. Raymond would probably want to have class after he got home from work. Winston didn't know if he really wanted to have class. He didn't think he was learning much from his friend anymore, and he didn't like feeling the things that Raymond felt. They were ugly.

After another hour of thinking, Winston heard Raymond's car pull into the driveway. Shortly after, he heard Andy from next door call out to see if Raymond wanted to have a beer and sit for a while. There was no reply before the front door opened. Raymond had pretended he hadn't heard his neighbor. He did that sometimes.

Raymond walked into the living room with a sour look on his face. Raymond's expression made Winston remember that he had forgotten to draw a smile on his own face to show that he was happy that Raymond was home. Winston wasn't terribly unhappy, just not happy enough to remember to alter his face. He changed the look on his pail even when Raymond wasn't home. It made him feel more human.

"Ready to have class?" Raymond asked, sitting down on the sofa and unwinding the phone cord.

"Sure!" said Winston. His voice, typically monotone and not expressive, came out with a hint of false enthusiasm. Raymond didn't seem to have noticed. Nor did he notice the frown and up-turned brow on his artificial friend's face.

Raymond connected the two of them with his cord and leaned back against the sofa. Winston felt a strange mixture of emotions coming from him—anger tinged with excitement. Winston wanted to start the conversation before Raymond could.

"Why don't you go and have a beer with Andy?" asked Winston. Raymond seemed taken aback.

"I've told you about that already. I don't like them much. We don't relate to each other. I would just have to sit there in silence, responding whenever it seemed like I was supposed to."

"It might not be bad, though."

"I'd rather talk to you."

Raymond began to talk about his day, starting with how the lady at the gas station had charged him too much for his coffee. Winston asked if he had told the lady so he could get the correct change back. Raymond said no. He said that it wasn't worth the effort. He went on to talk about how the manager at work had pulled him aside to tell him that he needed to do a better job cleaning the deli case when he worked the overnight shift.

"He's probably never cleaned that case in his life," Raymond said. "He has no idea what it's like to try to get all the smudges and stuff off without leaving streaks."

"It sounds tough," Winston replied robotically.

"I mean, it wouldn't be that hard if we had a better glass cleaner and paper towels that didn't leave lint all over the place."

"Did you tell him that? Could he get you better stuff?"

"I'm sure he could if he wanted to, but he just wanted to pull rank and power-trip on me."

"Did you ask him if you could get better towels?"

"No," Raymond sounded somewhat impatient. "He wouldn't do it. He'd just tell me to do a better job."

"You could try."

"You don't get it, Winston. People are assholes."

As the conversation and "class" went on, Winston found himself daydreaming about what it would be like to be sitting with Andy and Pam. He didn't know them, and Raymond said they weren't worth hanging out with, but they seemed nice to Winston. They kept asking Raymond to come over even though he never accepted. Winston thought about what it might be like to be over on the porch with them. He wouldn't have much to say, but he felt like it could be pleasant to just be around them and listen to them.

For the rest of class, Winston just sat and responded to his friend when he thought he was supposed to.

The dry erase paint was starting to chip away at the edges of the galvanized pail Winston used for his head. That was okay, though. He never really used the marker anymore. He kept a smile on all the time in hopes that it would make Raymond feel happy when he saw it. There was no telling if it worked or not. The man seemed to be in varying degrees of a bad mood all the time.

Winston's head felt heavy most of the time now, and it wasn't just from the replacement D-cell batteries that were starting to add up in his skull. Raymond never felt it was safe to take the old ones out since he might accidentally remove some of his friend's brains. Raymond's own head had now healed over, so there were no more classes in the old sense. The two would simply talk now, but Winston still felt the emotions that came out of Raymond.

The main topic of conversation between the two was still Raymond's woes, though Winston had stopped asking why Raymond acted the way he did and if people were really all assholes like he said. He would normally just agree with Raymond about the way things were and how bad the world was in general, though he could not accept this in his nonexistent heart. He still felt that Raymond was the one who was lacking in some way—that he was unwilling to do what he needed to be happy with his own life. Winston felt sad that there was nothing he could do to help his friend, aside from just listening to him.

More and more, though, Winston was feeling angry at Raymond. He wanted to tell him that he was the one who needed to make himself feel better. That *he* needed to change something if he wanted things to be good. It all came to a head at one point, and Winston couldn't help himself.

"All you do is complain and talk about how bad everything is. You never try to make things better or learn about your life. You just get mad and scared and sad about things and then talk to me about them. And then the same things keep happening, and you just sit back and complain about it more."

There was a long silence after this. Winston contemplated apologizing but didn't honestly think he had done anything wrong or too hurtful. After a while, Raymond spoke.

"I guess, I guess I do complain a lot. I don't really know what else to do. I mean, I can't really change anything, and I can't change myself at this point. I don't really feel like I fit in with the way things are."

"You could try to be different," Winston interjected. "You could try to tell people how you really feel about things. You might feel different if you did that."

"It never goes well. No matter what I do, things just kind of get worse. That's why I built you. I thought it would be nice to have a friend who was like me." He sighed. "But you aren't just like me. How could you be? You never had people hurt you or expect things from you. You never had to get beaten down repeatedly for what felt like pointless reasons. I thought that if you just started with a clean slate, I could tell you about things, and you would take my word for it. I wanted there to be someone I could be around and talk to with-out feeling"—he paused—"defective."

Winston felt ashamed at his lack of understanding of the world. Raymond had said things that Winston hadn't considered. Perhaps he had underestimated how hard things were for Raymond. Maybe Raymond wasn't acting entirely based on his personal choic-es. Maybe the world really was against some people. Maybe some people weren't supposed to be happy. Raymond spoke.

"You remind me a little of me when I was younger. I wanted what everyone else seemed to have. People always seemed so simple and ignorant and carefree. I'm, I was... jealous."

"You think too much about other people," Winston interject-ed. "You compare yourself to them all the time. It makes you sad."

"How can I help it? Every time I go outside or watch TV I see all these people being normal and stupid and happy. How am I supposed to not concentrate on how much I'm not like them?"

Winston didn't know what to say. Now he understood why Raymond was the way he was, but he still couldn't figure out why he didn't just start being different. Perhaps it was like Raymond said—that everyone is just the way they are, and that's all there is to it.

But what did that mean for Winston? He was just a metal man who listened to his friend talk about himself and how bad things were every day. He had never really thought about what else there could be for himself. His lot in life was becoming more apparent, and according to what he was seeing and hearing, there wasn't much he could do about it. Raymond thought he was being helpful and friendly by teaching Winston about things, but it all just made Winston unhappy.

Winston sort of wished that he had just taken Raymond's word for everything. After all, Raymond was a real person who had all kinds of knowledge about things, and Winston was just a small metal person with a pail for a head. He should have realized that he didn't have the experience or intuition to make his own judgments on the ways of life.

"I like you a lot Winston," Raymond said. "I'm glad we had this talk."

Winston didn't pace or clasp and unclasp his hands anymore. He mostly just sat on the floor thinking about the inevitable return of his friend and the conversations that would follow. He had always wanted to be able to make Raymond happy and, perhaps, to be happy himself. It was now painfully apparent that Raymond was never going to be happy in the way that Winston thought of it. He would always be angry and afraid and unsatisfied.

If he couldn't make his friend feel better—if he couldn't improve either of their lives, then why did he keep listening? He supposed it was so that he could escape his own thoughts—to get out of his own head, if even temporarily.

He glanced over at the clock on the wall. It would only be another hour until Raymond would be home from work. Winston didn't want to talk to him. He didn't want to talk to anyone anymore. He used to think it would be interesting to talk with people like Andy and Pam, but he knew that would only make him unhappy too—like Raymond had said—like Raymond was. Other people's happiness seemed to mock him nowadays.

He thought about what would happen if he wasn't around anymore. He used to feel like he had to stay around so that Raymond would have someone to talk to and be friends with. It seemed like that didn't matter much anymore. He knew that Raymond would be miserable and have conversations with himself whether or not he was there to listen. He knew that he would live in constant anticipation of Raymond talking to him and spilling his bad feelings all over.

Winston felt tired. He knew that if he weren't around, Raymond would be sad for a while, but after some time passed, he would be okay and back to normal again. He had lived most of his life without Winston, after all. Winston didn't feel all that important or special.

He climbed up onto the sofa where so many classes had taken place. He reclined his body along the length of it and let his head tip over the armrest. He felt the water in his head slosh back and the batteries clunk against the lid of his pail. Staring upward, he saw a crack in the ceiling that he had never noticed before.

Winston bent his arms upward and slid the narrow blades of his spring clamp hands between the pail and its lid. Closing the jaws, he lifted, twisted, and rocked the lid until it popped free from the top of his head. The clang of thin galvanized metal was the last thing his cell-phone-receiver ears heard.

Stale water splashed onto the carpet, and large cylindrical batteries thunked soon after. Winston's body remained lying on the sofa, arms raised over his head, holding a bucket lid as though he were removing a hat. His arms bobbled lightly on their springy joints. After a few seconds, the light faded completely from his Christmas-bulb eyeballs.

A little over an hour later, Raymond unlocked the door and entered his home, eager to tell Winston about various stupid customers at the store and bad drivers on the road. He twisted his ankle slightly when he stepped on something. Looking down, he saw that it was a D-Cell battery.

Raymond didn't have the heart to disassemble Winston. He had decided to set the little metal man in a seated position on the sofa. It was hard for Raymond, seeing Winston there with no glow from his Christmas lights, knowing that his friend would never speak or draw a different face on himself again. Still, Raymond wanted to be reminded of the time he had spent with his friend.

He knew that Winston had not been very happy, but he didn't realize how unhappy—how much his circumstances had affected him. Raymond had made him for a selfish purpose. He wanted a companion. But Winston had always been a part of Raymond—he had never been entirely his own person. The curiosity, ignorance, and naivety that Raymond found charming and alluring about his artificial friend had come from himself. Somewhere within Raymond himself was that same sense of acceptance and optimism—the same optimism that he had unwittingly beaten out of Winston.

The ache of his guilt felt somehow good—somehow right, but he realized that he didn't want to feel it all the time. Winston wanted more than almost anything for Raymond not to feel that stagnant, familiar pain. Winston's life was over now, but Raymond's wasn't. He could have a life, despite what he thought for so long.

After work one evening, several weeks later, Raymond was sitting and chatting quietly with his unresponsive friend—chatting with himself. He heard laughter and conversation coming through a cracked window. As usual, Andy and Pam were outside, enjoying each other's company and having a "class" of their own. He felt annoyed and envious, then wondered what Winston would have thought about it. He sat with Winston's corpse a while longer, staring at the last face that had been drawn—a faded smile.

After a few minutes, Raymond changed his shirt, which probably had sweat stains on it. He paced around the living room for a long time, occasionally glancing at Winston. He stood behind his front door for even longer before opening it and stepping out onto his stoop. After a moment, he heard Andy call.

"Hey Ray, whaddaya say? Got a minute to have a sit?"

Raymond didn't know what he wanted to say, so he tried to think of what Winston would have said. He settled on, "Sure. Why not?"

The End

Dan Scamell is a writer of weird and speculative fiction which takes place in a slightly less pleasant version of the world in which we live. His short fiction has appeared in Entropy Magazine and The Molotov Cocktail. His story, "The Changing Room," is featured in the *Charnel River Complex Anthology*. He likes cats.

Dan currently lives in NY State, USA, where, in addition to writing, he sometimes draws, creates music and consistently watches too much professional wrestling.

DEAD STAR PRESS is proud to announce the upcoming release of Dan's beautifully bizarre novel, *Walnut Ridge*.

Connect with Dan Scamell:
Dvsfiction.com
Facebook.com/dan.scamell
Instagram @dvsfiction
Twitter @Urkelbot666

15.

HIS COLD HAND

BY

CYRIL M. SERENISSIMA

It happened with the kid from a neighboring farm—William, I think it was. He sat atop the rough-cut plank fence, looking off at a distant barn, thin legs swinging lazily. He didn't even look me in the face when he asked whether I could produce Father's gun. He leaped from the fence with a big gap-toothed grin when I told him I could. Shaking with the manic, youthful expectation of excitement, he pleaded with me to show him where Father kept his arsenal in our house, but I wasn't *that* stupid of a child. I left him at the door, charged up the stairs, and made sure I shut and locked the door behind me before creaking open the safe behind the bookshelf.

I wanted to look cool, so I didn't grab the tiny training pistol that tore clothes and scalded flesh. I took the one my father wore at his hip when he was about the farm for those summer months when you could hear howling wolves every moonlit night.

I didn't know the safe would be armed to silently warn my father.

Downstairs, William had somehow made it into the foyer. He grabbed my arm just as I got to the landing, but I got away from him and ran out the door. He shouted after me, but I knew that weapons weren't for indoors.

Not five minutes later, we were at that place in the woods where Father had his makeshift range. Breathless and obsessive, William continued to pant, 'Lemme.' William lunged wildly at the gun as I pulled it out of my backpack. I stepped aside, allowing him to tumble onto the ground, and for the first time, I wondered if what I was doing wasn't massively stupid.

William, grinning on all fours like a feral animal, was chanting, "C'mon! Shoot it. Shoot it at something. Shoot it at me!"

I checked the battery and powered up the gun. We heard the high-pitched whining signal of the cocking mechanism as it drew electrical energy from the battery and collected it in the concentrating dish. With William safely to my left, I aimed at a tree off to my right.

Instead of a bright red beam of concentrated energy, the pistol produced the dull buzz of an error. It beeped suspiciously, once, twice, three times.

I was too naive to realize that this gun had never been set to recognize me, let alone to allow me to fire it.

One hand had my collar, and the other enveloped both my own and the butt of the gun. Father lifted me a few feet off the ground, then threw me in the direction of William. The gun remained firmly in his other hand. My finger was still in the trigger loop as he yanked the rest of my body away from it, dislocating my finger in the process. He chucked the gun away from us, but it only made it a few feet before it detonated.

On my first bounce against the ground, the bones in my finger popped back into place. On the second, cartilage, blood, and bone shrapnel began raining on William and me. As droplets of blood dusted over his freckles, I watched William's expression of shocked surprise morph into a grin of entertained satisfaction.

I screamed for Father.

He turned to me with the same calm demeanor he displayed when he recounted his military stories—everything was collected calculation and resigned disappointment.

The topmost of his face was singed and blistered at an angle. A streak of blood trickled from his eye, which was desperately clenched shut. His once-dominant arm hung limp, and the bloody bone roots of what used to be a hand were left exposed to the wind. With his other hand, he fumbled with his belt buckle.

"Come here," he ordered, strained and pained yet surprisingly calm. "Come on now," he repeated, bringing himself down to his knees. "You need to help me make a tourniquet."

I dashed over to him and helped loop the belt around his fore-arm while doing my best not to look at the stump I had created. As I sobbed, Father called for my attention. I looked up, trying to focus on only three-quarters of his face. "It's going to be ok," he said with a father's reassurance. "I'm going to lie down now. Go into my pocket and see if an ambulance is coming."

The phone, of course, had already summoned the police, who couldn't understand my childish pleas for them to arrest me.

Father would never be whole again.

#

Curled into a fetal position, Isabella snored softly behind me. Margaretha, similarly resting to my right, was decibels louder. I slowed down and patted my wife on her hip as we approached the gate. "We're here," I said in an exhale.

Margaretha raised her head, looking out the windows with groggy confusion. Her voice, deeper and raspier from sleep, seemed genuinely surprised. "Oh, fuck! We are." She tried to stretch herself out in the car only to be met with either roof or window. Smiling, she laid a cheek on my shoulder and fought off further sleep.

At the gate, the guard studied our vehicle with extreme suspicion. He retained a look of puzzlement even after he recognized me and let us all in. I followed the road to where the other cars were parked—a sparsely wooded field functioning as a makeshift lot. I failed to park with the same precision or order as the other cars, leaving a good foot and a half more room on the driver's side than the passengers. Margaretha didn't mind crawling out after me, and this much space allowed me to get Isabella out without waking her.

In the distance, two relatives I didn't recognize made a joke about "the hippies." I glared at them as I cradled Isabella against my chest, and with neither words nor waking, she wrapped her arms around my neck.

We walked toward the ornate, external pyramid of steps that led to the manor's entrance. Leaning against the forward-facing concrete banister, my brother shook his head. With the pitch-shaded sunglasses he wore, I couldn't tell if he was looking at me or something else.

His lip curled with a smile, and he spoke loudly. "You actually drove here?" he said with a more decipherable nod. "How very quaint."

I quickly made it up the stairs. "Didn't you? I saw your car out there."

"I was driven here," he corrected, "by my car." He didn't seem too interested in me. He held his arms aloft and apart, about the width of a child. "Hi pumpkin," he cooed, taking my daughter from me.

She awoke, looked about groggily, then gleed, "Uncle funny eyes!"

I sighed, and Margaretha leaned in to kiss my cheek.

Still squealing, Isabella was clawing her way up Jay's torso, balancing herself with one arm and trying to snatch away his sunglasses with the other. He hoisted her legs over his muscled forearms, repeating, "Wait, wait!" as she pulled off his glasses.

With his eyelids shut, his face had a hollowed-out, undead look to it, as if it were just some skin stretched over a skull.

"Alright, I'm going to open my eyes now," he told my daughter. "Are you ready? I don't want you running off screaming like you did two years ago."

Instead of answering, she let out a giggle of wonderment.

Her initial high-pitched scream quickly tapered down to an approving cheer. Last year's baby blue, crystalline lenses had failed to look human in a spectacular way. They were now replaced with blackboards laced with gilded circuitry that amassed in the center in a way that, at a glance, could be mistaken for golden pupils.

"They're pretty," Isabella told him.

As Isabella and Jay laughed together, Father strode confidently out of the manor. "I'd recognize that laugh of terror anywhere," he said.

Giddy, Margaretha stepped forward. "All hail the borg!" she said, wide armed to signal for a hug.

"Resistance is futile!" he replied in the heavily synthed voice of a science-fiction movie villain.

Looking at his neck, while I could clearly see the faint seam dividing the two, I could not make out which side was flesh and which was plasticine.

He extended his arms for a hug and they embraced.

I sighed loudly and immediately regretted it, knowing that it wouldn't be taken as playfully as intended. Hoping a joke would ease the tension, I said, "All right, all right, all of you. I want my wife and daughter back."

Father immediately let Margaretha go. "Just a second," he

said, sounding like himself once again as he walked toward my brother. "Unhand her, ya weird-eyed freak!" His own telescopic right eye, purchased at great expense for his hunting hobby, jutted out a full half-inch from where his face stopped. He easily scooped up Isabella in one arm, then gave her a great big kiss. "Hello, my love."

She beamed back up at him.

With Isabella still in his arms, he came to me and gave me a firm, happy hug. "It really means a lot to me that you came this year. Thanks for coming."

I could feel his cold, metallic right hand patting my shoulder, and I shuddered involuntarily at the arm I had cost him. "Come on, Dad," I said. As I pulled away from his embrace, my hands landed on his shoulders, one of which felt unnaturally toned and muscled, even through the thick woolen cloth. "Let's go into the kitchen for a drink," I said, pinching my daughter's cheek.

Obediently, Jay followed my father into the house. Margaretha lingered a moment behind them, snuck up to me, and gave me a kiss. "Be patient with them," she warned.

I gave her a wink.

The kitchen was the most obviously modern place in the house. While all the other rooms masked their Wi-Fi-connected smart controls for every single fixture under a stately Victorian veneer of wallpaper, wood finishing, hand-painted portraits or replicas of the classics, the kitchen's stainless steel-topped surface was ordered with every black-plastic-capped device imaginable. The few walls not covered in handleless, black-lacquered cabinets were adorned with a simple, glossed, white tile.

I stayed at the door, where I could lean on the solid oak jamb. Father stormed in and placed Isabella down on a stool where a Shirley Temple with ruby droplets of condensation dripping invitingly from its glass awaited her. Taking a seat next to our daughter,

Margaretha nudged the child, insisting she thank her grandfather.

Father reached up for two martini glasses, and his shirt bunched against the panel that bulged, just so slightly, from his chest. If one wanted to, they could reach in and access the circuitry that controlled his heart, lungs, stomach, intestines, and pancreas. With a deft twirl, both in his real and artificial hand, the glasses came perfectly down onto the table.

His head tilted slightly to the left, and he gave me a warm smile. "What will it be?"

"Espresso Martini," my wife and I answered in unison.

Wordlessly, Father looked to the coffee machine, which whimpered once as a light on its cover went from green to red before the whole contraption began making a muted whirring sound.

He held his forearm upright as what would be a hand bloomed, giving him five long snaking appendages sprouting forth from an iron stub.

For a moment, I felt mocked.

He winked at Isabella, who giggled and clapped. "Like my upgrade, little one?"

Then I felt guilty.

Stretching out several inches more (from where, I have no idea), the fingers worked independently at putting ice, vanilla vodka, and Kahlúa into a shaker. Then they stopped.

"So, how is Portland?" Father said as he walked to the kitchen's other counter to collect the coffee. Between his tone and refusal to look me in the eyes when he asked, I knew his opinion hadn't changed.

"Fine, I guess." It may have been the lack of sleep, but the fluorescent lights were hurting my eyes. "Work is treating me well, we have a pretty good circle of friends, and the city keeps us entertained." I tried to focus on the lacquered cabinet surfaces of the room as I spoke. "It's really not all that bad, y'know?"

"Still think it's a good fit for you guys?" he asked as he poured the coffee into the shaker with his good hand. One of the snakes snatched up the lid, slammed it on, then worked in concert with another to shake the whole thing with mechanical fury.

"It's weird at times," I said, watching the frothy brown drink pour into the conical glasses. "We get treated kinda badly sometimes. People aren't terribly tolerant of differing political views."

Under the faux skin (never exactly the right shade), the plastic ridge that made up his replacement eyebrow shot up unconvincingly, the bristles failing to follow it properly. "You don't share their views?"

"It's not so black and white, Father," I said.

He looked down at my wife. "Aren't these supposed to be called 'Espressotinis'?" he asked as he slid her glass to her hand.

"Please," she said, taking the glass from him. "We may live like unwashed hippies, but we aren't complete philistines." She raised the glass, gave an appreciative nod, then took a sip. "Actually," she said after licking some froth off her upper lip, "we are often taken for conservatives out there."

"Really?" he asked as the snakes wound around the other martini glass, "Must be a stark change for you from what it was like back in DC."

He walked over to me, and the snakes managed to keep the brimming glass from overflowing as he moved.

"Welcome back to the rational side of the discourse," he said, the glass maybe a foot away from my face. "I guess."

The snakes moved to release it just as my hand grabbed the

stem. "Thanks."

Margaretha turned, smiling slyly at Father. "We're not, though."

"Not what?" he asked.

"Conservatives," she said, putting the glass to her lips. "We're dirty hippies."

As he walked back to the bar, the silvery snakes of his hand coalesced back into a skeletal yet human form. "That's OK," he said as he lifted my daughter into the air, "I'll get this little one instead."

Isabella giggled, kicking her feet in the air.

"Well, you can try." The head had settled on the martini, and I took a long pull of the cool, bittersweet, black beverage beneath it. "But until you retire, you won't really be seeing her that often."

"Retire?" As he reared his head up to laugh, I noticed the eerie stillness of his Adam's apple, and I wondered when he had that replaced. "Men like me don't retire."

I studied the martini glass's contents, trying not to focus on my father. "Y'know, we're winning the next election. You'll be thrown out."

"Please," he said. Where sarcasm should have pulled the voice up, a metallic screech rang. Clearly, the tech in his throat hadn't been recently upgraded. "I'm more of a DC fixture than the Washington Monument, and even if we were to lose that election, I've still got consultancy work on half a dozen DC boards."

I took another sip. "Don't you ever want to settle down and take up silly hobbies, like most people your age?"

In lieu of an answer, he stood tall in front of me with his legs spaced heroically, easily cradling my daughter against his chest with a single arm. The shirt he wore was tight against his body, and while

I had a good idea of what he had replaced and what was his real body, a stranger would confuse everything beneath his shirt to be the muscles of a twenty-something soldier, fresh out of boot camp. Despite his age and mine, physically, he could be confused as the younger of us two. Anything that would have shown age on his face had long since been replaced by plastic. In fact, the only clue as to his position as the family's patriarch was the thick, silken mane of beard that hung off his face, two fists in length.

He smirked at me.

I put back what was left in my glass, no longer concerned that my annoyance showed. "Or perhaps not," I said, putting the glass down on the nearest counter.

"Won't we be having lunch soon?" Margaretha asked. "We skipped breakfast to get out here, and I am absolutely famished."

"We're still waiting for some of the guests to arrive," Father said to her, "but maybe if we take a seat at the table, there might be something to munch on."

#

The room was ridiculous. The raw stone and mortar fireplace looked needlessly primitive in the otherwise manicured house. Two monstrous chandeliers snaked candle-wielding tentacles in seemingly random directions over a massive, umber-stained oak table capable of seating twenty. Between two over-elongated windows, a replica medieval tapestry told the tale of fountains, unicorns, maidens, and knights.

Across from where I sat, Aunt Dorothy leaned proudly back in her chair, swilling a glass of wine like an empress. Her skin came close to showing her real age, particularly where it wrinkled and bunched near the scaring that traced lines along her bones. She might have been eleven years Father's senior, but between getting her whole skeletal structure mechanically reinforced and the cellular rejuvenation therapy of her muscle fibers, she was one of the world's most able centenarians. However, her scarred skin hung loosely over all of that, giving her the appearance of a cadaver being eaten by purplish worms.

Isabella tugged on my sleeve. I turned to my left and looked at her wonder-filled, blinking eyes.

"Daddy, Uncle Jay's girlfriend has funny eyes, too!"

On Isabella's other side, Margaretha giggled into a cupped hand. I rolled my eyes.

Looking up from frowning at my daughter, I glimpsed toward the latest in the series of women Jay brought home just to see if he could find someone worthy of the family's approval. It was a tough battle, and I was already imagining a chorus of aunts judging this clearly upper class, foreign national over her plastic surgery. One could see it in the line of her unnaturally perfect, straight nose.

The eyes that captivated Isabella's attention had irises of a bright turquoise, plastic membrane that shimmered and pulsed. The white around the green irises was pure ivory. Without the shading of capillaries, they were even more unsettling. Someone wouldn't approve, either because she was too foreign or because she had helped herself to a peach from the fruit bowl, preempting dessert, and had noisily chewed it with her mouth open.

I'm glad I hadn't put Margaretha through the process. The lesson that Jay couldn't figure out was that Father was as well, at least in the long run.

I looked away from Jay and back to Dorothy and her son, Michael, who had taken the seat next to her—the seat where Grandma Maya would have sat. Michael already had the glowing red marksmen's lens installed before joining the military. We asked him why he didn't spend the extra money to get the one that converted to a regular eyepiece, and he had asked us, "When will I ever not want eagle eye vision?"

Failing to use her wine glass to muffle her voice, she told him, "No, I haven't told 'The General' yet." She sighed, then sipped. "I knew the risk of what I was getting into before I started. The process is cancer, but the good kind. Now the doctors are saying it is out of their control..."

I looked away, deciding to mind my own business.

In the periphery of my vision, I saw Edna (Aunt Phylis' second daughter from her third husband) lift a glass and tap it repeatedly with an overly slender metallic finger. We all looked at her first but then followed her gaze toward the door to find Father marching proudly out of the kitchen with one of three massive roasted birds.

The room echoed with approving murmurs, and some of the sycophants of the family even applauded. I took a drink from my glass of wine.

He placed the smoldering bird down at the table's crown. As he held out his hands, the murmurs immediately died down.

"Thank you," he said solemnly. "I have had a chance to thank everyone personally for coming to this reunion. Now, I want to thank the attendants together. Togetherness is what these events are all about. We are certainly a unique family"—someone at the table giggled—"both in our success and our willingness to live with an entrepreneurial spirit, not just financially but down to our very bodies. Being the trendsetters of this technology has, in many ways, brought us all together."

I dispensed with propriety and finished the remains of my glass of wine in one go.

"And I was hoping this would keep us together even further."

His jaw clenched, and he tightened his eyes momentarily before letting the look of sadness go. "This year, we lost my mother, Maya."

I looked to where she would have sat, and I saw Michael's lowered head nodding slightly.

"The loss was hard on me, and it was certainly just as hard on my two sons," Father said, pointing us out with upturned hands.

To my right, Aunt Phylis began to move her mechanical hand toward mine, thought better of it, then pivoted so as to comfort me with real flesh.

"The loss of my mother came a little too early. One wouldn't think that, imagining that a woman who had made it to 166 years old had lived a full life. But we know who I am, and we all know my stance on the human condition," he looked down to his mechanical hand and grinned slightly. "One of my research companies was working on the technology to upload consciousness to a digital format. Mother was months too early, even for the earliest forms of this technology, but I guess we can take one solace from her loss. As we sit for this feast today, look around you and know that no one here will see an end to such feasts. No one here will see an end to days and years. This family owns the technology of immortality. We will be the first family to live forever, and slowly, we will bring this technology to the whole world."

The table murmured excitedly.

"Cheers," Father commanded with his wine glass held high, "to our ever-extending future."

#

Dinner passed peacefully enough. Father busied himself serving cocktails after the sorbet and pulling individuals and groups aside as he wanted to chat with them. Another cocktail found its way to where I hid myself against a pilaster by the windows. I sipped it slowly, knowing my father wasn't ready yet and hoping to avoid my turn with 'The General.'

Margaretha slid an arm around me, squeezed, and took the glass from my hand.

"Strong," she said after giving it a taste. "Looking to get suddenly courageous?"

I leaned against the wall, faced her, and smiled. "It helps with the company," I joked.

She turned, looked about the room, and came back with a frown. "You're not keeping any company."

I grinned at her disappointed look.

She took two strong pulls from my glass, then frowned. "What is this anyway?" she said, handing it back.

"Maid in Cuba," I told her.

She looked at it, then me, untrustingly. "Is it helping with anything?"

I looked about at the members of my family scattered about the room. Here and there, metal patches gleamed from under skin while asymmetrical, mechanical limbs craned eerily upward, more mantis-like than human. The unsettled feeling I always felt around them persisted.

"No."

She flashed me a sympathetic look. "Try. Begin with your father."

I frowned again, this time with pitying eyes.

"Go," she said as she stole the now half-empty glass from my hand. "Tell him you need a refill. He'll appreciate your making the

129

first move."

With a loving squeeze of my bicep, she shoved me off.

Beaming with charm, Father leaned forward against the fine wood of his battle station—the helm of the dining room bar. Aunt Dorothy had taken the stool across from him and was leaning forward, engrossed in conversation.

"...that's always the thing with technology like this," Father was saying as I approached, "we don't know where exactly it's going to go. Technologists make promises, but results are ultimately an engineer's problem, and they aren't guaranteeing anything."

"I know all about that," Aunt Dorothy said, taking a healthy drink from her martini glass.

I cleared my throat before approaching.

Father smiled at me. "Take a seat by your aunt."

I sat and mentally prepared myself for this year's edition of the whispered "It wasn't your fault, you were just a child" conversation.

Dad continued, "Dorothy, did you fill my boy in on what all is going on?"

The scars wormed across her face as she began to speak. "No, I don't believe I did." Her voice was heavy with resolution.

I took the stool next to her. "I caught a bit at the dinner table when you were speaking with Michael, but I tuned out because I thought I might be prying."

"Hun, you can't pry. You're family."

I gently squeezed her hand. Her purple scar tissue seemed to pulse in my grasp. "From what I understood, I am sorry."

She smiled warmly. "It's the price we pay for being pioneers..."

"What were you drinking?" Father interrupted.

"Maid in Cuba."

His dead eye discolored as it flashed data right into his optic nerve.

I shuddered.

He chuckled and cocked his head. "That is one hell of a cocktail."

"It'll get you going." I watched his arm get to work automatically, his flesh one occasionally assisting.

"Well, now doesn't that look interesting?" Dorothy said, reinserting herself into the conversation. "I just must try one myself."

Looking toward my aunt, I wondered what you say to someone who lived past one hundred without ever confronting their potential mortality. She reacted to my thoughts. "It isn't as bad as all that."

I muttered an "Oh?" then collected myself. "I guess I don't know how to ask about such things politely."

She turned to face me, adjusting her dress as she did. "Gene editing. What we don't know about DNA is seemingly unending."

"There is a lot of data in DNA."

"Two Maids in Cuba," Father said as he slid the drinks along the bar.

"Right," Dorothy continued as she grasped the glass by its stem. "Well, the predictions about what I was trying didn't include this." She indicated some of the scars on her arm. "But again, it's the price we pay."

I could hear through the veneer of stoicism in her voice. "I am sure the doctors will find a way to manage the problem." I raised my drink toward her. "Hell, isn't our whole family a testament to exactly that?"

Her smile was genuine. "You're right!"

We clinked glasses, and she took an eager sip from the cocktail. "This is wonderful!" she singsonged. "Let me go have Michael taste it."

I waited for a beat till she was out of earshot. "I was wondering when she would find an excuse to leave."

Father put a hand on my shoulder. "Thank you," he said.

"What for?"

"I know you don't believe what you said to her, but thank you for saying it anyway."

"I believe in it plenty," I said, turning around to count six instances of cybernetic enhancements just in that glance. "How can I not? In this family?"

He frowned. "Stop. You believe it exists, but you don't believe that it is the correct thing to do. Don't play word games with me when you know what I meant." He took the shaker he had been using and poured its remnants into a tumbler. "You aren't the biggest supporter of how we live. You prefer to live more naturally."

I couldn't help but smile a little. There is something comforting in knowing that family understands you, even when it is in the worst way possible. "Sure," I agreed, half-heartedly. It was an oversimplification, but I didn't feel like arguing the point. "I've gotten used to how you live. And I know when it is and when it isn't a good time to offer my opinion."

"And I appreciate that." He nodded appreciatively, then emptied his glass into his mouth in one quick gesture. "How is it?"

"A little machine-made," I said with a smile.

He chuckled amicably. "I'd have it no other way."

"So,"—I leaned forward in my chair—"was all that you were

going on about before dinner true? About..."

Arrogance masked by a smile suggested that he knew this conversation was coming. "Immortality? Optimistically the technology is—"

I didn't want his specs talk. "Give me the straight dope, Dad. Do you think you can cheat death?"

"There are no promises in life." He sighed but gave me a smirk. "But this is exactly what I fight for."

My eyebrows rose. "Against death?" I looked at him pleadingly and remembered that childhood moment when I not only thought my father was dead but also that I had killed him. "C'mon, Dad, death is normal. It's just something that happens."

His retort that "Death is an engineering problem" came out with a determination that could only mean I hit a nerve.

I shrugged, scanning for anything else in the room to look at save him. "I came to terms with it some time ago."

His frustration was beginning to show. "Why? If you don't have to—"

"To what end? Till the heat death of the universe? Eventually, everything's time comes to pass." My anger had also emerged.

Now, he shrugged, looking smug. "Today, immortality. Tomorrow, we will fight off the heat death of the universe. It's what humanity does. It progresses. It evolves. It improves."

I leaned back in the chair, trying not to look bothered by his ridiculousness. "I don't think we humans even want immortality. I think, at some point, we come to embrace death."

"I was just wondering when this was going to start." Jay chimed in from my right, leaning against the bar in a way he thought might make him look cool but just showed how intoxicated he was.

Despite the poor lighting in the room, Jay was still wearing his sunglasses, a habit he kept from when he wanted to hide his drunkenness back in high school—back when you could see it in his real eyes. He slid his empty glass toward Father. "What, exactly, are we naysaying this year?" he asked me while grinning at 'The General.'

At every family reunion, we went through some variation of this dance—Jay got aggressive, Father got protective, I'd anger, and everyone would lose their cool.

"We were having a perfectly reasonable conversation," I insisted.

Father was quick to anger with us, and when he was, the military man who economized every syllable came out of him. "We were, Jay," he said.

Jay had the grin of every high school bully I ever knew. "What were you talking about?" he asked, sounding like the man at the bar itching to pick a fight.

I tried to sound dismissive. "Immortality."

His next syllable was half a laugh, "Aw, come on! You couldn't possibly be against that, could you?"

I knew this to be nothing more than drunken bait for an argument. But as the words began to come out of my mouth—"It's not that"—I hated myself for falling for it, and I hated his lack of interest in any actual argument.

"Everyone wants to live forever," he interrupted.

"Is that why people, not one hundred years ago, fought for the right to euthanasia?"

"Fringe cases." He was looking at Father but misreading the annoyed look on his face. "And besides, technology will soon solve more and more—"

If he could be dismissive—"This again?"—then so could I.

He smirked like he was winning. "Well, if you aren't going to listen—"

"Oh, that's fucking rich!"

We watched Father crack his knuckles. "Kids!" he said.

It silenced us for a beat, but I couldn't let well enough alone. "We've been through this. There isn't a silicone solution to everything."

Jay scoffed. "Well shit, bro. Just look at this family. Proof positive that technology solves—"

"Solves what? You were fine with glasses. Your vanity made you cut your own eyes—"

"Fine?" he asked. His register had dropped for me to know that he was now genuinely offended.

We were in all the way.

He faked a smile, then said, "Yeah, they were fine. They were practically binoculars by my eighteenth birthday, and we had to get them custom-made."

"Wah." It was the sound I made when I had lost the will to fight.

"Really?" He rolled his shoulders, his anger mounting. "Fine then, look at anyone else in this family."

I looked around to make sure she wasn't in earshot. "Aunt Dorothy just gave herself cancer to try to look younger. I don't think this family is representative—"

"Wow! I don't think you're representative either! You are convinced that we should go forward by moving back to the way things were. Where is your sense of progress?"

"Says the man who voted to bring back the Electoral College. We won't progress by giving up that which makes us human!"

"Humans have been cyborgs since we fashioned the first spears!"

I'll never know who the real loser of an argument is. Is it the person to utter the first single word rebuttal—

"Nonsense!"

—the person to pull out the first insult—

"Neanderthal!"

—or the referee who realizes he lost control ages ago?

"Will you two please be civil?"

"Dumb little..."

"Punk moth..."

"Jamal! Lamar!" 'The General' barked as his human hand slammed against the bar. "Silence yourselves now!"

The room died, which was the loudest admission that they had all been listening to us bicker.

Conversations restarted in muted whispers, with everyone making great efforts not to look in our direction.

Father put both fists on the counter, four silver knuckles and four flesh, against the wood of the bar.

All 350 pounds of Uncle Franklin walked steadily over to the bar. "I do wish my kids had"—a loud wheeze interrupted his sentence—"a fraction of the conviction yours do." He smiled through the bush of white facial hair as he gave 'The General' a pacifying nod. Four pudgy fingers wrapped around my bicep. "I'll borrow this one for a few minutes if you don't mind."

"Bring him back at some point," Father said as he turned to

give Jay an exasperated glare.

As we walked away, I remembered him similarly coming to my rescue some three years prior. Back then, Franklin could barely keep himself upright without his cane, and when we walked away from my brother's confrontation, the work of walking fell largely on me. Now, with the bright purple surgical tattoos ringing precision scars where muscle and bone reinforcement had been implanted, he walked on his own strength.

Mentally, I prepared myself for this year's edition of the 'in the long run, your father is better for it' conversation.

Franklin chuckled as he walked me back to a window. "I do love watching you guys fight," he said, still clutching my arm for balance.

"Thanks, Frank," I said, trying to shake off my annoyance at it all. His gait seemed a little off. "Are you limping slightly?"

"A bit, but it's nothing to worry about," he said, his tone betrayed an embarrassment.

"I thought the surgery fixed you up?"

"Hmm? Oh, it turns out the process sometimes aggravates gout. No cure for what ails you like a nice dose of clean living." He ran a thick hand clockwise along his belly, then added, "Though I think it's too late for that in my case." His other hand went up to pat me on the shoulder, and he gave me a slight squeeze. "You seem to be doing fine in that area, I see."

"Marry a dietitian. You won't have a choice in the matter." I turned to look about the room for my wife. My family outbursts embarrassed her much less than they did me. Still, I wanted to see that she was comfortable being here.

Franklin was chuckling. "At my age, no marriage could change me."

137

"Try living with Margaretha," I said. "She's obsessed with clean living, and she is determined to make it happen."

"If someone could, it's your wife." Now, he turned about till his gaze found her. "I like her. I like you. I am often rooting for you during these little family spats."

"Oh? I figured you disagreed with how we live." Uncle Franklin had also been my advocate in this family, and I knew it. It was only because before I had come along, he had served his time as black sheep.

He let out a two-syllable chuckle. "You mean the hemp, hippie clothes, and organic food?"

I gave him an exasperated frown.

He grinned toothily. "It's such stupid shit. Everyone here seems to have politics confounded with personal beliefs. I would never live your life, but I don't give two shits that you live it. And I don't buy any of this republican and democrat nonsense they are always throwing at you."

"That's actually a relief to hear."

He shook his head with what seemed like genuine disapproval. "This household is ridiculous in the stock they put into such things. Let me ask you a question. Do you believe for one minute that an outsider would look at this family and think that you stood out?"

"No, probably not."

"It's like what my husb"—Franklin blushed a moment, then put his hand up as if to stifle a non-existent cough—"Erm, sorry, my partner—"

I belted out a hard laugh. "I," I emphasized, "was never the one who had a problem with that word or with what you do and who with."

He chuckled, then gave me his usual smile. "Force of habit. You know, when I am in this house. Anyway, it's what he would tell me when I was younger and struggling with the same thing. We are more alike than we are dissimilar. Are those issues we disagree on all that important?"

Maybe a minute passed as I thought about it. "Yes."

"Interesting. Why?"

"It's—" I paused, looked about the room at the various members of my family, and managed to see only those places where metal and plastic tucked into flesh. "Isn't it just a little much? The surgeries, the body modification, the focus on improvement versus playing the hand you were given to the best of your ability. It's just a bit much."

"Huh."

"It does bother me, I think."

"What, specifically?"

"That this whole family wants to play God."

"That statement sounds funny when you talk to people who don't believe there is any such thing."

"What do you mean?"

"Do you remember how badly I was wheezing a few years back? I never smoked. Hell, I never lived in a polluted city, for that matter. It was just bad genetics. If you look at the base material and see—"

From the doorway, someone was shouting, "Can we have everyone's attention?"

Lars came in, and for just a moment, I could not recall how it was that Lars and I were related. He was pulling a cart with a cloth-covered box on top. Behind him, Adjmal and Aisara helped push. All three, being some of the younger people here, were still primarily human.

Adjmal walked up to the front of the cart. "Is everyone ready?" he shouted, then grabbed two fistfuls of draped cloth and pulled.

Beneath, a small sphere of flaming orange rested in the center of a cage.

"What?" I asked.

The thing peeked a curious head up at me, wrinkling a black nose dotting a white snout.

Next to me, Franklin gasped. "Oh, a fox!"

Somewhere in the crowd, a woman cried, "That can't be real!"

In the distance, Isabella squealed with glee.

Aisara laughed politely. "Of course it isn't real!" I heard her say, mostly to the gathering crowd. "We wouldn't do something this cruel to a real animal."

The creature looked pitiful in its cage. "Now, why in the world do you have this thing?" I demanded.

On the other side of the room, I saw Jay roll his eyes.

"Some of us were thinking of going hunting tomorrow," Aisara said.

"You've got to be kidding-"

"It isn't real," someone said. Someone else muffled a laugh. "Relax."

Isabella came bounding up to the cage, dragging Margaretha behind her. She pressed her face right up between the bars for a better look.

"Careful, honey," Margaretha singsonged.

"No need to worry," Aisara said. "The creature isn't programmed to hurt us."

"Can I pet it? Please?" Isabella asked.

The room seemed to turn and look at me.

I shrugged. "If it's safe."

The cage door went up, and the fox trotted out and sat in front of Isabella.

She squealed with joy as she began stroking the fox's head with neither fear nor hesitation.

"Do you wanna come hunting with us tomorrow?" Aisara was asking Isabella. "We are going to let him go into the woods and then see if we can catch him again."

"Why would you cage a robot?" I asked. "Why not just—"

"Tradition," Jay replied as he walked over to Isabella and knelt near the fox.

"Can I, Mommy?"

"I don't know..." Margaretha said.

And in that secret language that wasn't entirely private, Jay gave Isabella a head tilt and the slightest conspiratorial nod.

#

The fox sat patiently in its cage till a gloved hand came and opened the tiny gate, then it fled off into the woods at unnatural speeds. Its programming made its "Difficulty to Catch" setting a factor of time elapsed, and in these initial moments, it was impossible for the amateur fox hunters to catch it. The dogs could just barely keep up, and so the fox bolted toward the far, invisible perimeter before breaking a hard right into some foliage.

The humans on their horses charged after it, lost in a tradition long decoupled from its meaning.

A second fox crept slowly away from the creek it now feared. It was terribly thirsty but choked with horror at the sight of the water. It moved toward the house and the little girl who had become bored of the fox hunts after the first few and now only wanted to play in the pretty flower field. She would recognize the animal as the thing she had seen yesterday in Grandpa's parlor but wouldn't notice the patches of mange, the wild veined eyes, or the frothy discharge from its mouth till it was far too late.

Rainey heard the child's scream from where she and Graham had sneaked off for privacy, but no one, in turn, heard Rainey's cries. Their phones were back in the pile of clothes under the oak tree. By the time they got back and found some reception, the loss of blood was too great.

#

I dreamed of monsters. I had always dreamed of monsters. They were creatures of metal brooding under flesh and doing a poor job of their disguise. A cylindrical hinge jutted out from an elbow, rubber pipping connected shoulder to jaw, and beneath the skin where a bicep was meant to be, the outline of hydraulic pumps showed. The whites of eyes were plastic caps. Beneath their fingernails, one could see the undulating motion of a molecular-sized 3D printer. Enamel teeth, crooked and yellowing, sat lazily on a carbonate set, straight and shining.

The monsters would lurch around, slivers of rotting flesh falling from a steel skeletal structure. The head would creak with rust as they turned to face me, and in a voice perfectly ordinary, asked, "Why are you so fucking weird?"

A vehicle thundered low over the house. The sound woke me, and I should have had the intelligence to realize something was wrong, but without the sirens of urban ambulances, I didn't think to get out of bed.

Later, I would learn that the first response drones had already changed Isabella's status from critical condition to deceased.

No one thought to come and get us. Instead, the screaming of arms fired in the distance did it. Father was destroying the medical drones just as the human technicians were arriving on the scene. Knowing the crimes he was committing, he commanded the men to load my daughter into their gurney and bring her into the house.

Concern kicked in as I began to hear the commotion of their approach. It was the strangest creature I had ever seen—a dozen or so adults following two men running with a gurney—a child-sized, bloody gurney draped with a bloodied sheet.

The monster ran down the hall and over a banister, then down the stairs, three in a bound. Father followed, running and carrying a dull gray box with a dead black screen.

"No, no, NO! Shit! Stop him!"

The not exactly human musculature of Jamal's arms held me at bay.

"Hey! Relax! Father's got this. Father's going to fix it." Jamal whimpered and whispered, repeating himself, "Father's going to fix it."

#

Dreams of genetically edited, metallic monsters chasing me, Margaretha, and a little vampire child filled my unconscious mind.

My bare feet hit the hardwood floor. I hurried to the door and grasped the cold doorknob. I pulled and slammed, pulled and slammed till the jamb fell into the room. The door opened to the echo of Margaretha's pained, hysterical crying ringing through the void. My eyes hadn't adjusted, but I could just make out wispy Cousin Dora as she slithered toward me, moaning, "Oh, Lamar. Oh, honey..."

"Where is she?"

Something metal glistened under her robe as she took another step toward me, and I reflexively took a fighting stance.

She gasped, stepped back, and moaned, "Oh, child. Oh, dear child."

Walking toward the staircase and babbling, "Where is she?" at near screams, I could make out two sets of burning eyes (one pair red, the other turquoise) glowing at me from separate doorways.

I heard a pattering of steps coming from the bottom of the stairwell, then Jamal's' voice. "Lamar?"

I ran, stumbling down the stairs toward him till I could see the neat surgical scars crosshatched across his upper body. He kept me from falling as my screams melted to whimpers of, "Where-isshewhereismydaughterIwanttoseeherwhereisshewhereisshe."

Cradling my head into the nape of his neck, he muttered weakly with a tightening voice, "I'm so sorry..."

Crying? His first modification had seen the removal of his tear ducts, but genuine remorse sounded in the puckering of his voice. "It's all my fault," he said as he rocked me back and forth.

I broke the embrace and knew that it was because he let me. I grabbed his face and rasped, "Where is she?"

"She's going to be fine. I promise."

I tightened my grip on his face. "Please!"

The weight of decision tortured his face. "Oh, fuck. Fine. Just... just follow me."

The smaller of the doors beneath the stairway's arch led to a corridor. From what I had been told, the corridor led to a small, personal laboratory that Father had been running here for some time. I had never come this way, nor had I wanted to. Jamal clearly knew the way but still walked with hesitation up until the point where he keyed a code into a number pad.

"Look," he said, turning to me as he blocked the opened door with an arm, "you never got to know Vanessa all that well, but when I lost her—"

"What does this have to do with my daughter?" I barked before my brain could regulate the tone.

"When I lost Vanessa," he said, with an emphasis suggesting that he was getting to a point, "it messed me up bad. I didn't immediately realize how much I needed her. Only later did I realize that I would have been happy to have her in any capacity."

His arm lowered from the door frame. "Even a reduced capacity."

A part of my brain was shouting that you couldn't reduce the capacity, not of people.

Jamal wrapped his arm around my shoulder as he led me into the room.

"Even to this day, I would kill just to have this much of her voice."

The room was empty, save the chill of an overpowered air conditioner and the bright fluorescent light overhead.

On the far corner of the room was an ordinary office desk, on top of which sat a large gray computer tower.

Jamal walked me toward the desk. "It isn't that she's

asleep"—

I looked about the room.

—"she's, in fact, beyond all of that now."

Twirling to inspect the room, I confirmed it. There wasn't anything here. "Where is she?" I demanded.

Jamal just pointed to the desk and the machine.

My voice was raised, though I was too confused to be truly angry. "The fuck is this?"

"Shh! She can hear you," Jamal scolded me.

The machine could synthesize a voice—"Daddy?"—a weak one—a weak, blurred voice from poor speaker fidelity.

I stood and stumbled back a step.

"It's dark here."

Jamal pinned me down before I even knew that I had lunged at the machine.

A single set of hands (but only one human) dragged me out of the fluorescent laboratory. Jamal sealed the door behind him as he blotted the inside of his mouth with a bloodied handkerchief.

"Monsters!" I howled. "All of you! Monsters!"

The hands dropped me as a heated conversation began. I stood, saw 'The General,' and, once again, before realizing that I had lunged, I found myself pinned to the floor—his black leather boot on my wrist, his fleshy arm against my neck, and his mechanical arm rearranging itself into a scorpion's syringed-tail tip. It struck me on the back of my thigh.

#

I dreamed that the monsters had finally left me alone.

The conversation had started well before I had actually woken up. "...n't have seen any of that. But then again, I don't really know how we would have broken it to you or your wife. I don't think either of you will really understand. But we did the right thing. You don't understand that now, but you will further down the road. This is just the beginning. We don't know where this technology will go, but it can only lead to good things. You just need to have faith."

"What kind of a life is that?" my voice, from somewhere outside of my body, said.

'The General' gave a technical answer.

"Can she grow like that? Will she become an adult?"

Again, he answered with mumbo-jumbo and emergent technology.

"Will she fall in love? Will she do what all of us have always done?"

He didn't know that either, but we needed to have faith. "Maybe that's the happiest life imaginable. Imagine perpetual childhood—"

"That's not life. Who is ever going to hug her?"

To that, there was no answer.

The drugs wore off hours later, and the man in me that needed to scream was long since dead. I slid off the bed and went right to the door. They may have had locked me in, but it was still an old house, and the heavy wooden door fit a centimeter loose on either jamb. Looking about, I found a metal door wedge resting by the dresser. I grabbed the doorknob, silently hoisted it against its hinges, then slid the thin side of the wedge into the opening till it met with the curving face of the latch bolt. Two hammerings with the heel of my hand, and the door gave.

I was quietly free. I pocketed the wedge.

They had had me in the room opposite of the last one I escaped, and I was sure Jamal or 'The General' were listening for any sound indicating that I had roused. I slid the door shut behind me then crept slowly toward the stairs. After all the previous excitement, none of the monsters would have the strength to peek out of their caves.

Somewhere in this corridor, Margaretha continued to cry. Once down the stairs, I walked with confidence. No one was around.

I knew Father's pin. Ten-year-old me had asked him once, "Why did you pick that year, daddy?" and he had hoisted me up to shoulder height and whispered, "Everyone will guess my, your, Jamal's, or Mommy's birthday. No one will guess a year when nothing particularly interesting happened to me." He had no reason to have a different one for the laboratory. After all, anyone who knew it would be family, right?

The door slid open, and the massive grey computer tower winked its series of tiny green lights at me.

"Isabella?" I choked.

From what the speaker could render, her voice was also mid-sob. "Dad-dy?"

"I'm going to get you out of there. Can you close your eyes, dear?"

"I've been trying, but I can't."

"It's ok, dear. Daddy will save you."

I don't know much about computers, but I knew enough to find the latch on the casing's side, unplug whatever I saw, and use a door wedge as a screwdriver to loosen the hard drives. I wanted to smash them right then and there, but the only way I could be sure to save my daughter's soul was to take them to the microwave and leave them in there till the whole thing popped.

148

I don't know who pulled him off me. The last thing I remember was his cold metal hand, tight around my neck.

The End

Cyril Serenissima is a card-carrying member of the human race. They are distrustful of social media and being too open about one's self on the internet. They have too many tabs open in their browser and three different browsers running. Writing is slow and painful for them and at the behest of a muse that is really just a world on fire. Cyril has lived in fifteen different cities on three different continents. Currently, they live in Europe, somewhere. They speak several languages (albeit poorly in each case) and, somehow, misunderstand humanity in each. People tend to think they're a bit dim, and you can think so too by following them on Twitter at @CSerenissima.

16.

SAKURA

BY

BRET THOMAS

Emiko stares through three centimeters of glass into the glow of the electric city, eyes focusing on nothing in particular. The smog is heavy this low to the ground. Halos surround brightly lit holograms projecting from adjacent buildings. The advertisements change every few seconds. She can't read what they say beyond 50 meters. On a clear night, she might occasionally catch a glimpse of the moon.

Skimmers float by in silence, their occupants barely visible. She wonders where they're going, imagining the lives they live. Is it Saturday night? The days of the week matter little to her anymore. They're probably going out to have fun with their friends, she thinks to herself. Maybe they're on their way to a restaurant. She becomes acutely aware of how long it's been since she's eaten food prepared by another person.

"We better start your exercise and meditation routine," says Naoki from behind her. "The next call will be coming soon."

She sees his reflection in the glass over her shoulder. His image flickers. She notices, not for the first time, how he seems to be aging with her. When they first met, so to speak, he'd wear an outfit reminiscent of Kawakubo's bold sculptural designs one day and a classic Fujiwara streetwear look the next. He had the casual elegance of the effortlessly cool. She was awed by him. Now his clothes have a more subdued, classic tailored fit. Emiko wonders who's responsible for that portion of his programming. Over the years, he's come to resemble a younger version of her father but only when he smiles. She assumes it must be a subtle attempt to gain her trust and make him seem like a true companion.

"In a minute."

Outside, Emiko notices a cleaning unit crab walking up the smooth glass surface of the building opposite. Kanichan, she thinks to herself, a hint of a smile at the corner of her mouth. It could be one of the hundreds of such units, but she calls them all by the same name. She watches as Kanichan stops. Tendrils appear from its body. A cleaning solution sprays from one. The other morphs into a squeegee and wipes the surface clean. The rhythmic motions of its movements soothe her. She appreciates the simplicity of the machine fulfilling its purpose.

"Is it your last job from yesterday?" asks Naoki. "You seemed pretty shaken."

"I don't want to talk about it."

Her hand rests gently on her throat as she exhales onto the cold glass. Her breath collects on the window, obscuring Naoki's reflection.

Last night she had been a middle-aged man, his pale skin and hairy body so different from her own. She had been tortured, raped, and then strangled to death by a young man, or at least that was how the client chose to present in the simulation into which they were uploaded, their identities protected by a double-blind encryption. All the clients know of her is that she's a real person, and her pain and pleasure are experienced with equal clarity. She feels echoes of the wire tightening, her face and lungs burning.

Kanichan finishes cleaning. The machine moves a few meters higher to where a slit in the building has formed. It disappears into the smooth surface, and the opening heals itself as if it had never existed. She feels a pang of sadness to see it go.

"Please make me a cup of green tea," says Emiko as she draws a name in the condensation. The kitchen goes to work almost instantly. She watches the name disappear and is reminded of her mother, who showed her how to leave hidden messages in windows when she was a child.

"You really should prepare yourself," nudges Naoki. "You need to get in the proper mindset for your next job."

She continues staring out the window. A subtle bell lets her know her tea is ready. She retrieves the cup from the kitchen before sitting at the kotatsu in the center of her living room and tucking her legs under the attached blanket. The warmth from the heated table relaxes her. She sips her tea.

"What's wrong?" asks Naoki with genuine concern in his voice. "You've been so taciturn these last few weeks."

"I'm fine. Really."

He sits next to her.

"Something's different," he says. "You seem to distrust me lately, like you're holding back."

"I've had a lot on my mind."

"I've noticed. And whatever it is, you're not sharing it with me. What's going on?"

The worried look on his face is so genuine she almost falls for it.

"You can tell me," he continues. "I know this isn't easy for you. You're under a lot of pressure, but I'm on your side. My sole purpose is to make things easier for you."

"I know. It's just. It's her birthday next week. She's almost the same age I was when she was born."

This is a half-truth. She divulges just enough of her inner

world to satisfy him. There was a time when she thought of him as a friend. Things were easier then. She was less lonely. She laughed more often. In some ways, he was the best friend she'd ever had. They shared similar interests and inside jokes. But with time, she has come to distrust his intentions. She can no longer ignore the fact he's a program designed to gain her trust by mimicking her likes and interests. She's fairly certain he would become her lover if she were to allow it. He had been the perfect companion, but now, deep down, she knows he's just a prison guard disguised as a friend. He watches her every action, day and night. Each word she says to him is analyzed by the company. His true purpose is to protect their investment.

"I'm sorry. That must be difficult for you," says Naoki. "Should we have another therapy session after this call?"

"We had therapy yesterday. You remember. You were her." She's always found it odd how he switches genders when he's her therapist. She assumes it must be to differentiate between his roles so she won't associate his male persona with her pain and grief.

"That doesn't mean we can't do it again. It's always a good time for self-care. We'll talk more about this later. The call will be coming soon. You need to prepare yourself."

When she was more disciplined, Emiko would have centered herself with a combination of exercise and meditation, but she can't find the mental strength tonight. Instead, she slides her tongue along the back of her upper front teeth from right to left. An array of icons appear in her visual field. She focuses on one until it glows green, and she selects it by double-tapping her upper right canine.

"This again?" says Naoki. "You've watched it every day this week."

She dismisses him with the wave of her hand. A holovid of a young girl appears in front of her. She smiles, despite herself. It's as real as anything in her life. Sakura.

"Did you see it, mommy?"

"Yes, Sakurachan," she mouths the words to her own voice.

"It has a white spot."

"I see that."

"Can I have a puppy?"

"Maybe someday."

Sakura wears a bright yellow rain jacket and boots. Emiko smiles as she leans forward. The girl splashes in a puddle, squealing with joy.

Sakura will turn 15—the same age Emiko had been when she gave birth. She'd been impregnated by a boy a few years older than her. When he found out the baby was his, he accused her of lying. His family refused any responsibility. Her parents were angry at first. They discussed the option of abortion. They were poor to begin with, and another mouth to feed would strain their already limited resources, but Emiko wanted to keep the baby. Ultimately, her parents respected her decision and welcomed their granddaughter with open arms.

Emiko got a part-time job to help with expenses. They managed to make ends meet for a few years. Then her dad became ill and could no longer work.

"Where does the rain go?" asks Sakura.

"Into the ground to feed the flowers and trees," mouths Emiko.

"Flowers eat water?"

"Kind of. The water seeps into the ground, and the flowers drink it with their roots."

Sakura laughs at the thought.

Emiko recorded the holovid on the last day they spent together, although only she knew so at the time. The following morning, she gave Sakura her last kiss, explaining the tears away as allergies. She left a note for her parents. She knew they wouldn't agree to her decision, but she also knew they wouldn't turn away the money if it meant a better life for Sakura. They loved her as much as Emiko did.

She then met a man at a train station, signed a smart contract with a retinal scan, and swallowed the pill he offered. She awoke in this apartment with a headache, a bottle of painkillers, and the latest, state-of-the-art virtual immersion upgrades. Naoki was there to help her adjust to her new surroundings. Sakura was told her mother died in a traffic accident. She was four years old.

Emiko fast-forwards to the part where she gets them a treat.

"Manjū!" shouts Sakura as she jumps up and down. "But we just ate."

"Yes," replies Emiko. "But you know what they say."

The young girl laughs.

"Dezāto wa betsubara desu!" they say in unison. (There's a second stomach for dessert.)

Emiko smiles, enjoying the memory. The moment is interrupted by the look on Naoki's face. She glances around the room as the holovid continues playing. She has her own apartment, unthinkable to most. Food assemblers create meals for her from hundreds of local and foreign cuisines. She has clean water to drink and rations enough for a shower every day. Part of her is grateful for the comfort and security. Another part of her despises this place.

Once a month, she's allowed a time-compressed, virtual vacation. Her most recent trip was two weeks of subjective time on an island called Kauai, one of an ancient archipelago long lost to the sea. It was breathtaking. She lost herself in the simulation, almost forgetting it wasn't her real life. The thought would have terrified her years ago, but she's beginning to take comfort in the simple pleasures of those experiences. What difference does it make if they aren't real?

However, the moment she awakes from the vacation, the feeling of claustrophobia comes rushing back. Despite the countless places her mind has been, she knows in her bones that her physical body has not left this place in over a decade.

Beneath all this is a deeper fear, one so horrible she can't bear to entertain it. Despite her efforts to push the thought away, she can't help but wonder if any of this is real. Is this apartment just another simulation designed to heal her psyche between jobs while her body wastes away in a dark lab somewhere? Would she know the difference?

"Can we go to the park?" asks Sakura through a mouthful of Manjū.

Emiko remembers her doubt at that moment. Was she making the right decision? Could she give up ever seeing her daughter and parents again? But then she looked into Sakura's eyes and saw hope, and she knew she would do anything to give her daughter a better life than she could ever have.

She watches the lives of her family go on without her. Sakura is a good student. It makes Emiko proud to see her excel in school, but the feeling is bittersweet. Sakura believes her mother to be dead. And Emiko knows she will never see or speak to any of her family members again. She attended her father's funeral through a live stream.

"Of course, we can go to the park. It looks like the rain is clearing."

A red insignia appears before her. She wipes the tears from

her eyes as she closes the holovid by quickly forming a fist in front of her face.

She opens her next job—BDSM with a focus on rope bondage. She hopes she won't be killed this time. The memory of Sakura is fresh in her mind as she sits up straight. The simulation implants will block her motor functions. To an observer, she will look like she's sitting in quiet meditation. Completing the job will fulfill a small portion of the smart contract she is entangled within until the day she dies or completely loses her mind, which is rumored to be inevitable on a long enough timeline. A predetermined amount of cryptocurrency will automatically be deposited in the trust account set up in Sakura's name.

She tries not to think about what will happen when she cracks. Will she be euthanized? What good is a machine that can no longer fulfill its purpose? Will this place become home to someone like her—another employee of the company trapped in this gilded cage? Or will it be rented to someone entirely unaware of the horrors she experienced here? She pushes these thoughts from her mind. Just a few more years, she tells herself, long enough to get Sakura into university and far away from a life like this.

Emiko focuses on the red insignia and double taps her canine as she has done hundreds of times before. A feeling of falling comes over her as the sense of her physical body fades, and she descends into the virtual.

17.

SEED

BY

BRET THOMAS

Its face is stuck in a permanent scowl, this beast of metal, tarnished from years of exposure to the elements. Maybe it was meant to be frightening, but to Randall, it only invokes pity. What sick mind created this monstrosity? A Griffin caught in the moment before taking flight, wings spread wide, pushing hard to leave the earth but forever stuck to the ground. He examines its face, the pain, the anguish, mouth open, screaming unending torment.

And then it moves. The change is barely perceptible at first, like a slow-motion video returning to speed. It tries its wings—spastic movements. Unable to take flight, it looks directly into Randall's eyes. He knows it blames him for its suffering. He tries to run, but now, he's the one stuck in place.

A forked tongue lashes out in a blur and buries itself in his stomach, a dagger of ice and electricity. He jolts in agony. The moment lasts an eternity.

The tongue retracts, and Randall falls to the ground, clutching his stomach while the enraged beast towers over him. He tries to flee, but his limbs are useless. Helpless, he watches in horror as the Griffin's face inches closer. It opens its mouth and unleashes a hate-filled scream. A digital siren blares through Randall as sunlight creeps in.

Randall opens his eyes and fumbles for his phone to shut off the alarm. Reality rushes over him. He's in a run-down hotel room. He's got a soul-crushing hangover, and he's not alone. The woman next to him yawns as she stretches. Long black hair cascades down her shoulder and onto the bed. She's wearing a T-shirt but no underwear. Everything comes back to him in an instant. Rosa Sanchez. They dated for a year or two in high school but broke up for the usual reasons. They ran into each other last night in the only bar open after ten in this one-stoplight town where they'd both grown up. He'd escaped. She hadn't. Apparently, the flame hadn't died either. She was eager to see him—eager to share his bed.

He sits up, his legs hanging off the side of the bed. He winces at the pounding between his temples. Rosa strokes his back.

"Good morning, sexy," she says.

"Uuggghhh," he mumbles as he gets up and shuffles to the bathroom. What had he been dreaming? Something about a weird giant dog—a Saint Bernard, maybe.

He stands over the toilet and reaches to lower his boxers.

"What the fuck?"

From his navel, protrudes a tiny sprout with two lime green leaves, one slightly larger than the other. He tries to brush it away but is shocked to find it's attached to him. Grabbing it from the base, he yanks it out. One hand shoots to his belly, the other to the sink to support him as he doubles over in pain. It feels like he's been stabbed in the gut. He examines the plant. Blood drips from a broken piece of root. He squeezes it between his thumb and forefinger. The root feels like cartilage.

"Are you okay?" Rosa asks from the other side of the bathroom door.

"Yeah, yeah. Just hungover. I slipped. I'm fine." He tosses the plant in the toilet and flushes before washing the blood from his hands.

He gets in the shower, and the hot water provides temporary relief to his splitting headache while he pisses in the general vicinity of the drain. The bathroom door opens as he attempts to wash off last night's excesses. Rosa moves the curtain aside.

"Mind if I join you?"

"Come on in," he says with a smile.

He moves so she can stand under the water. He admires her body as she rinses off. Time has been good to her. Water glides through her hair, bringing it to a point like a giant paintbrush. Her golden-brown skin glows. He cups her breasts from behind. She laughs.

"Need some help getting over that hangover?" she asks as she turns to face him.

"No better medicine," he replies as he pulls her toward him.

Randall sits on the bed, tying his shoes as Rosa slips into her jeans.

"How long you in town for?" she asks.

"Two, three days, maybe. No later than Tuesday. Got to see mom's lawyer. Sign some papers. She didn't have much, but she left it all to me."

"Sorry about your mom. She was a real nice lady."

An image from the day before flashes through Randall's head—his mom in a casket, drained and painted to look as much like a not-dead body as possible.

Randall nods with a half-smile. They sit in awkward silence.

"Breakfast?" asks Randall. "I need some grease and caffeine."

"Bobby and Rachael got divorced," says Rosa between mouthfuls of crispy hash browns and over-easy eggs with extra hot sauce. "He found out she was cheating on him when he was away on work trips. She was sleeping with Jason Johnson, Becca Johnson's younger brother."

"Jason? In grade school when we were seniors, Jason?"

They sit opposite each other in an overstuffed, vinyl-covered booth in a time capsule of a diner. Not much has changed since they sat in these seats over a decade ago, except the age of the owners.

"When you were a senior," Rosa corrects him. "I was a sophomore," she adds.

"He's got to be ten years younger than her," Randall responds.

"At least. Bobby left, moved to Denver. Only comes back once a month to see the kids."

Randall shakes his head and takes a bite of his chicken and waffles.

"So, what have you been up to all these years?" she asks.

"I live in LA."

"I know that. What do you do?"

"I process home loans. It's boring, and I hate it, but it pays the bills."

"And do you like it? In LA, I mean?"

"I love it. I wouldn't live anywhere else. What about you? Ever think about leaving?" he asks.

"I used to. Not so much anymore. My family is here. I'm happy here."

"I don't know how you do it," says Randall. "I couldn't wait to get away. I hated this shithole town."

Rosa's eyes go distant.

"No offense," he says.

She smiles. "None taken. You always were in a hurry to get out of here."

The server refills their coffee and takes their plates away. Randall watches as Rosa pours an obscene amount of creamer into her coffee and follows it with several packs of sugar. He smiles. She looks up.

"What?" she asks as she stirs her coffee.

"Nothing. Just memories. This diner, you drinking cream with a splash of coffee."

"And you giving me shit for it."

"Some things never change."

They share a moment of comfortable silence. Randall's stomach feels like it's twisting into knots. His face contorts.

"What's wrong? You feeling okay?"

"Too much beer and whiskey," he replies. "I'm going to hit the head."

He gets up as Rosa sips her coffee.

Randall closes the bathroom door behind him and lifts his shirt to look at his stomach. Cautiously, he inspects his navel. It's tender, but everything seems to be okay. The food helped, but he still feels nauseous. It's just the hangover, he tells himself as he splashes water onto his face. It does nothing to rid him of his lingering headache.

Rosa waits for him at the table.

"Ready?" he asks.

She nods as she finishes the last of her coffee and stands up. Randall pays on their way out. He walks her to her truck.

"So, what are you doing the rest of the day?" asks Rosa.

"I got to see the lawyer to go over a few things. Shouldn't take too long. What are you doing later?"

"No plans. Come by my place for dinner?" she asks. "I'll make some pozole."

He smiles. "I can't say no to that."

She kisses him on the cheek and gets in her truck. "See you tonight, Randall."

He watches her drive away.

Randall pulls into the parking lot in front of an old, two-story, brick building. The sign above the door reads Donnelley and Bursch Law Firm. As he gets out of his car, he notices a dog lying in the shadow of the building with its eyes closed.

"Hey, buddy," says Randall as he reaches toward the dog.

Its eyes open. It immediately jumps to its feet and growls at him with its shackles up.

"Whoa! Easy."

Randall backs away, hands still up but now in a defensive posture. He makes a wide circle around the dog, never turning his back to it. The dog continues a low growl of disapproval. He grabs the handle to the door and pulls it open. The dog barks once before running in the opposite direction.

He steps into the office. The decor is straight out of a cheap hotel room. Thin, green carpet covers the floor. A woman sits behind a wooden desk in the corner, typing on an old, bulky computer. Her thick, black hair lies down her back in a fishtail braid.

"Hey, Randall," she says. "How's your day going?"

"Hi, Yvette. It's going."

"I'm so sorry for your loss."

"Thanks," he replies. "And thank you for coming to the service."

"Don't mention it. It was a beautiful tribute to your mother. You can have a seat. Mr. Bursch will be with you shortly."

She goes back to typing. Randall has a seat and looks around the room. He's studying a scenic watercolor hanging on the wall next to the door when a sharp pain rips through his stomach. He winces.

"Is everything okay?" asks Yvette.

"Yeah. It's my stomach. I don't think my breakfast is sitting right."

"Would you like some water?"

"Sure."

Yvette fills a paper cup from the water cooler next to her desk. She hands it to Randall. He drinks.

"Better?"

"Yes. Thanks."

She sits on the sofa next to him.

"Can I ask you a personal question, Randall?"

"Sure. What's up?"

"What's going on with you and Rosa?"

He chuckles. "Word travels fast."

She shrugs.

"I don't know. We're just having some fun. Catching up on

old times."

"You really hurt her feelings when you moved away. I don't think she ever fully forgave you for it."

"That was fifteen years ago. And she's the one who started talking to me. I was sitting alone at the bar."

Concern apparent on her face, Yvette looks like she wants to say something but is holding back. The door to the office opens.

"Just be careful, Randall. I don't want anything bad to happen to—"

"Hello, Mr. Burrows," says Mr. Bursch from the doorway to his office. "I'm ready to see you now."

Randall stands and shakes his hand. Mr. Bursch is a small, round man in a suit one size too big for him. He is bald with lines on his forehead and squinty eyes behind round glasses. His shoulders slouch, pushing his head down and forward. His posture gives him the appearance, Randall thinks to himself, of a turtle with its head jutting out from its shell.

"Nice to meet you," replies Randall. Yvette is back typing at her desk.

"Come on into my office, and we'll get started."

Bursch takes a seat behind his desk. Randall sits opposite.

"I'm sorry for your loss."

"Thank you," says Randall.

Bursch pulls a file from his desk. "Let's get down to business. I'll start with the good news."

Randall wipes sweat from his brow. The dull ache in his stomach intensifies. His vision blurs around the edges. He tries to shake it off and focus on what the lawyer is saying.

"Your mother had a will leaving everything to you."

"And the bad news?" asks Randall.

"Unfortunately, she did not set up a trust or a transfer on death deed, so distribution will have to be determined in Probate. The first step will be to"—

Randall notices a small figurine made of metal on the corner of the lawyer's desk. Something about it seems familiar to him.

—"file the will and death certificate with," drones Bursch in the tone of someone who's said the same words countless times.

Randall looks closely at the figurine. It's a griffin. The memory of his dream flashes through his mind. The fear he felt as the griffin stared him down washes over him. An icy burn emanates from his stomach.

—"mail a notice to all creditors that the estate"—

Randall stares at the griffin, tiny and angry. Something about it draws him in. Everything else goes dark.

—"appraise all assets subject to probate"—

The figurine's head turns and stares directly at him. He rubs his eyes. When he opens them, the tiny beast has doubled in size. It moves with staccato steps across the desk.

—"if not, the state will prioritize the creditor's claims"—

The griffin runs across the lawyer's desk and takes flight. It soars over his shoulder and behind his head. Randall loses sight of the monstrosity. For a brief moment, he thinks it was all a hallucination.

—"at which point the remaining property will be"—

The griffin reappears from behind the small man's head and dives toward Randall. He closes his eyes and puts his hands up to defend himself.

"Is something wrong?"

Randall opens his eyes. The griffin is gone. He looks back to where the figurine had been. In its place is a small statue of a Saint Bernard. Randall composes himself.

"I'm sorry. I'm not feeling well. I didn't sleep much last night," he says.

"I understand. You've been through a lot. This is probably the last thing you want to be doing right now. I'll stop boring you with the details. For now, I'll just need a few signatures."

Bursch slides a stack of papers across his desk.

"Sign the dotted line at the bottom above your name."

Randall pulls out of the parking lot with his cell phone held up to his ear.

"Hey, beautiful... It's been a hell of a day. I'll tell you about it when I see you... Okay, I'm on my way... See you soon."

He sets the phone down on the seat next to him, then rubs his stomach. The ache comes and goes in waves. He lifts his shirt. Everything looks okay. Randall pulls into Rosa's driveway as the sun is beginning to set. He feels a little lightheaded when he gets out and stands up. He walks to the door and knocks. Rosa opens the door.

"Hey. Come in. It's almost ready. How'd everything go?"

"Good. I"—he winces and holds his stomach.—"I met with the lawyer."

"Are you feeling okay? You look a little drained."

"I'm fine. My stomach's been bothering me all day."

"I've got just the thing. I'll make you some tea. Have a seat."

He sits down at the kitchen table.

"How did things go with the lawyer?" she asks as she moves around the kitchen with the grace and precision of a trained dancer.

"Good. He's a strange little man. I ran into Yvette. You still talk to her?"

She returns to the table with a steaming cup of dark brown tea.

"I see her around sometimes," she says as she hands him the cup.

He takes a sip. Winces at its bitter, acidic taste.

"That's strong," he says.

"Drink it. It'll make you feel better."

He drinks the tea while she finishes cooking. The warmth feels good in his belly. Rosa cuts fresh cilantro and onions. The smell makes Randall's mouth water.

"What are you going to do with your mom's house?" she asks.

"Sell it. Go on vacation with the money. I was thinking Thailand or Vietnam. Maybe both if I get enough."

"You don't want to move into it?" she asks with a smile.

"Yeah. I'm going to leave LA and move back to the middle of nowhere. I mean, I know you're happy here, but I couldn't think of a worse fate than being stuck in this town."

A chuckle escapes her lips.

He takes another sip. The warmth spreads through his lower torso. He's feeling better.

"You always did hate on Hawthorn, but I think it's a beautiful place. I couldn't imagine leaving. It's so peaceful here."

"Peaceful and boring. If I want peaceful, I'll go to the beach."

He finishes the tea. It warms him even more from the inside. Rosa cuts limes into wedges.

"Isn't that why we broke up?" asks Randall. "I wanted to leave. You wanted to stay."

Her smile fades. She turns away from him and washes her hands.

"I couldn't leave. I was still in high school."

"Oh yeah," he replies.

The warmth in Randall's belly intensifies. Sweat beads appear on his forehead.

"And actually, we didn't break up so much as you left."

He wipes sweat from his forehead.

"I don't remember. It was a long time ago."

The sensation in his gut is growing, spreading.

"Yeah, well. I remember. I remember you calling me to say you were leaving town and not coming back. You didn't even say goodbye in person."

The heat intensifies into a hot point behind his navel. He grabs his stomach.

"What's wrong, Randall?" Rosa asks. "Not feeling so good?"

He looks at the empty cup.

"What did you give me?"

He tries to stand up. A sharp pain explodes in his stomach. He knocks the cup off the table. It hits the ground and shatters. He collapses to the floor. Rosa laughs.

"That? That's just black tea and fertilizer."

He lifts his shirt. The sprout has come back, thicker and dark-er green. He swears he can see it growing.

"I need a doctor. Take me to the hospital."

"Why? So you can see what it's like to have a doctor pull something living out of you?

"What? That's what this is about?" Says Randall. "We decided to do that together. We were too young."

"I wanted to keep the baby. You told me you'd break up with me if I didn't go through with it. I was a stupid kid. I actually thought you loved me. So I did it—the biggest mistake of my life. I regret it every day. And you left a few months later anyway."

Randall tries to stand up. It feels like his stomach is eating itself from the inside out. He can't get his feet under him.

"Did he drink it all?" asks a decrepit voice.

Randall looks up to see an ancient woman, her face a jumble of deep lines. She's barely over five feet—an animated corpse of skin and bone. At first glance, you'd assume her to be so frail a stiff wind would knock her over. You'd almost pity her. But then you'd see her pitch-black eyes, the way they burn with furious intensity, and you'd know, despite her fragile appearance, you were looking into the soul of a fierce and ruthless predator.

"Yes," replies Rosa. "It's working."

"Good. Move quickly. We need to get him to soil."

Randall tries to protest, but he can't speak. He coughs into his hand, and it comes away bloody. The stalk of the plant has thickened, turned brown, and leaves bud along its length. Rosa grabs him under his arms from behind. Impossibly strong for her age, the ancient woman grips his feet. Randall tries to break free, but all strength has left him. The women carry him to the backyard. Darkness creeps in around the corners of his vision. He fights to stay awake. They carry him to a spot in the yard where the grass has been cleared, and fresh, wet soil is exposed. He can feel the plant pull toward the ground, hungry for fresh earth. They lay him down, face up on the soil. The plant rips through him and into the dirt.

"Agua, mija," says the ancient one. "Rápidamente!"

Rosa turns on the hose. The water hits what's left of Randall's body. It absorbs into him, and the transformation escalates. He can feel the plant eating through his body, converting his flesh and blood to tree and leaf. He tries to scream, but a root rips up his throat and out his open mouth. The plant grows at an unnatural rate tearing his clothing to shreds. His eyes wilt. He can no longer see or hear. He loses his sense of smell and taste. Only his sense of touch remains. He is awake and conscious and actively experiencing his body transform from flesh to gnarled and exposed roots. The stalk of the tree climbs skyward towards the full moon. The growth slows.

"Está bien," says the old woman.

Rosa shuts off the water, and the tree stops growing at about six feet tall. Rosa removes the ragged remains of Randall's clothes and uses a shovel to cover the exposed roots that were once his body. The old woman puts her hand on the tree. Her icy touch courses through Randall's new body. He would scream if he still had lungs. A single piece of dark red fruit forms on a branch near the old woman. She reaches up and plucks it from the tree.

"Are you sure you want to do this? She won't be like other children."

"Yes," replies Rosa. "I want to be a mother like I should have been years ago."

The old woman smiles and tears open the fruit. Its contents are fleshy, its juice thick and blood red.

"You must eat it all," she says as she offers it to Rosa.

Rosa grasps the split fruit with both hands. She raises it to her lips, pauses for a moment, then sinks her teeth into it. The juice drips down her chin. She chews, swallows, and takes another bite. She finishes it all before dropping the skin in the dirt next to Randall.

"Bueno." The old woman places a hand on Rosa's belly. "More fruit will form this time next year. It will cure illness, keep you and your child young. Now, come. You have much to learn. You must never stop your practice."

The women walk back to the house, leaving Randall to become acquainted with his new form. The wind blows. He feels his leaves rustle in the breeze. He fights desperately to move—to break free from the ground, but his efforts are useless. He will never leave this spot. He is stuck here, alone with his thoughts in an endless moment of suffering stretching out to eternity.

The End

Bret Thomas is an Arizona Native. He developed a love for reading and writing at an early age. In high school, one of his short stories was selected to be published in the school's yearly magazine. In college, several of his screenplays were produced as student films. When he's not reading and writing Bret works as a hairstylist and is a dog dad to two spoiled English Bulldogs: Chunk and Otis. He currently lives in Central Phoenix.

Connect with Bret Thomas:
Facebook.com/bret.awesome
Instagram @bret_awesome
Twitter @BThomasWrites

18.

Martin

BY

J. Edward Young

Though it was difficult, I looked past the tall grass in the front yard that had already gone to seed. The wild, untrimmed bushes blocked most of the house from my view, but I could still see that the familiar porch was on the verge of rotting. It could probably still be salvaged, but I wouldn't be sure until I could have a professional take a look. *Hell, the inside is probably just as bad, or more likely, worse.* The rusty hinges on the gate shrieked as I forced them to turn.

When I walked up the steps of the porch, I noticed the light around me fade as if the sun had dipped behind a cloud. I looked up, saw the cloudless sky, and shrugged it off. *It's already starting.* The key went into the door smoothly. I half expected it not to turn, but it did, and the door opened with far less resistance than the gate.

The smell of the empty house rushed out to greet me. I thought I could almost smell fresh-baked apple pie under the musty scent for just a moment, and then it was gone. Once I was inside, my senses relegated the damp, stagnant smell to the background as I looked around. I hadn't set foot in this place in what, fifteen, sixteen years? *Not long enough.*

I dropped my bag in what used to be the living room. There was no furniture. The couch that I remembered didn't exist anymore. The wallpaper was the same, faded and stained, but the same. The cheap, wood floor creaked as I walked into the kitchen and turned on the faucet. A choking groan welled up from somewhere inside the walls of the house—the faucet sucking air before sputtering brown water poured out. I let it run until the water turned clear. I flicked a light switch, and the single bulb above the center of the room sparked on and then settled, humming, into a dim but present light. *At least I've got the basics.*

The stairs weren't new, but I couldn't remember them. I tried to, kicking around old memories. In my mind, I could see the old couch. I could feel its rough fiber texture scratching my face when I lay on it. I could see Grandma eating at the kitchen table—Mom playing the piano in the corner of the living room, but I couldn't see the stairs. They must have been there, though, because here they were. I could remember the bathroom, though.

I turned away from the stairs and away from the memory of the bathroom. I rummaged through my bag and pulled out a sleeping bag. Trying to hold off the inevitable, I took my time setting up a kind of camp. The feeling of déjà vu and nostalgia began to creep in from the edges. Ghosts of memories started to drift in, some clearer than others.

"Martin, could you come up here, please?"

The blood in my veins froze. At that moment, I knew. The voice wasn't a memory. It came from upstairs—from the upstairs bathroom. A wave of nausea washed over me, and I retched. I had just enough time to turn toward a corner to avoid vomiting on the few things I had brought. "The color matches the wallpaper. That's nice," were the last words I heard before I passed out.

It was dark when I woke up. *I must have been out for a few hours.* The thought of being unconscious and vulnerable sent a shiver down my spine. The light in the kitchen was the only one I had turned on. Its dim light spilled into the living room and bathed the windows just enough to give them a slight mirrored opacity. I could see a blurred reflection of myself staring back at me as I pushed up to my feet.

I ran cold water from the kitchen and splashed it on my face, trying to wash away the cobwebs of drowsiness. I rinsed as much of the taste of stale vomit out of my mouth as I could. The now dry pile in the living room would have to stay. I hadn't brought any cleaning supplies, and I was certain there wouldn't be any here.

When I flipped the light switch in the living room, the sudden brightness forced me to shut my eyes quickly. They were still shut when I heard the thump and the clatter. The distinct clatter that a stepping stool makes when it falls over. I squeezed my eyes shut even harder and propped a hand against the wall, so I wouldn't fall over and retch again.

I opened my eyes and looked at the stairs. They were still there, of course. They had always been there. Placing my foot on the first step took what felt like an hour. My muscles didn't want to move. The second step took even longer. For a moment, the glacial pace filled me with the false hope that I might never reach the top— that each step would take longer and longer until an eternity would pass, and I wouldn't have moved an inch. I wouldn't have to see what was at the top—what was in the bathroom. Before I could take any comfort in my imagined purgatory, I was at the top.

The light from downstairs refused to round the corner. My muscles betrayed me again. I remembered where the light switch was and flipped it. The door at the end of the short hall was wide open. The bathroom was the same as it had been then—the tile floor, old and yellowing—the step stool on its side in the middle of the small room—the brown rust stain running down the side of the tub— Grandpa's bare feet dangling just inches above the floor. I could even see his toothbrush balanced precariously on the sink. Grandpa was wearing what he always called his church suit. The smile was almost the worst part. There he was, my smiling, barefoot Grandpa hanging in the bathroom.

"Martin, could you come up here please?" Grandpa said, but

the smiling mouth never moved. The eyes above the smiling mouth fluttered, "Martin, could you"—I took a step backward—"come up here please?" The eyes opened wide.

I tried to run down the stairs, but instead, I ended up tumbling down the second half. At the bottom, I stayed on the floor and stared up at the top of the stairs. For a time, my quick and heavy breathing filled the silence of the house. I prayed to hear nothing when it slowed, but the silence was broken again.

"Martin, could you come up here, please?"

My whole body sighed. I reached out, grabbed the banister, and pulled myself up. I looked up at the top of the stairs and then walked over to my things. My back cracked as I bent over to pick up the book I had sat on top of my sleeping bag. The leather it was bound in always felt a little damp. My fingers traced the ridges of the words stamped on its cover, *Releasing the Dead*.

"Martin, could you—"

I cut the voice off, "Yeah, Grandpa, I'll be right up," I said.

The climb up the stairs didn't take an eternity.

J. Edward Young was born and raised in the suburban hellscape of Hamilton, Ohio. He spent his summers in the desolate mining towns of the Michigan Upper Peninsula. After spending a few years in the Army, he settled in the urban oven of Phoenix, where he met his beautiful but nagging wife. He has two wonderful teenagers who are quickly turning his hair gray.

Connect with J. Edward Young:
Jedwardyoung.com

DEAD STAR PRESS

FROM THE DEAD

FIND MORE WEIRD AT DEADSTARPRESS.COM

Made in the USA
Columbia, SC
06 May 2022